Unspoken Social Rules & Etiquette, (Un)common Sense, & How to Act

By Patrick King
Social Interaction and Conversation Coach at
www.PatrickKingConsulting.com

Table of Contents

Part 1: Making Contact 5
   Chapter 1: Greeting and Introductions 5
   Chapter 2: Etiquette in Public 19
   Chapter 3: Eye Contact Etiquette 29
   Chapter 4: Small Talk Danger Zones 37

Part 2: The Golden Rule is Respect 51
   Chapter 5: Punctuality Is Respect 52
   Chapter 6: The Power of Respecting Other's Opinions 63
   Chapter 7: Respecting Personal Space 75
   Chapter 8: Having Respect for Boundaries 85

Part 3: Unspoken Rules of Engagement 97
   Chapter 9: What the "Flow" is and How to Go with It 97
   Chapter 10: Honoring the Rule of Reciprocation 111
   Chapter 11: Gratitude, Manners, and Kindness .. 123
   Chapter 12: Humor Etiquette 137

Part 4: When Things Don't Go to Plan 149
   Chapter 13: Navigating Social Misfires 149
   Chapter 14: The Art of Saying NO . . . Nicely 161
   Chapter 15: Apology Etiquette 173

Summary Guide 186

Part 1: Making Contact

Treat everyone with politeness and kindness, not because they are nice, but because you are.

–Nicole Wharton

Chapter 1: Greeting and Introductions

You might think the word "etiquette" is hideously old fashioned. In a world that more highly prizes individual personal expression and authenticity, it can seem like social rules are an outdated and repressive piece of history we've all moved on from. However, if you're reading this book right now, there's a strong chance you suspect that this is not true—and never has been.

Human beings are social at their core. But the paradox is that socializing doesn't necessarily come easily or automatically. Enter social rules about how we have all agreed to behave in social situations. True, these rules are never written down or taught at school, and yet we all know they're there—particularly when we break them!

In the chapters that follow, we'll not only explore the very real and very important rules that hold the shared social fabric together, but we'll also look at exactly how to put them into practice in a world full of ambiguity, grey area, and imperfect people. Can a person live without all these unspoken social rules? Maybe. But by the end of this book, you may find yourself proving just how much of an advantage you can give yourself by mastering them. Becoming socially adept makes life easier, richer, and far more rewarding. **The rules, you will see, don't restrict human expression and flourishing, but enable it.**

If you're the kind of person who wants to be more likeable, a better communicator, and more skilled at diffusing misunderstandings and conflict, then read on.

Every culture on earth, at every historical period, has unanimously agreed on one thing: At the start of any encounter with another human being, people need to say *hello* first! The Victorians made a high art of introductions and greetings, placing enormous weight on what was said, how, to whom, and in what order.

Today, more relaxed and modern cultures have fewer rules about how to open any social interaction.

But there are always rules.

This chapter may seem a blindingly obvious place to start, but the sad truth is that many people *think* they understand this basic fundamental skill . . . and still get it wrong. **The biggest mistake? Simply forgetting to greet at all.** Yes, even if you are shy or consider yourself an introvert, are nervous or are having a bad day. Yes, even if you feel awkward and don't know how. Yes, even if *they're* the ones being rude first.

Every greeting and introduction are a chance to show respect for the other person and give them a good impression of you. There's a reason people say first impressions matter—it's because they do! But one thing people forget is that first impressions are not just a chance for you to show who you are. They are a chance for you to graciously demonstrate that you are willing to have a good impression of the *other* person.

It's worth dwelling on this point. In ancient times, when humans encountering a stranger was a rare and potentially dangerous situation, the tone they set in those first few seconds made all the difference in the world. **The very first task in any social situation is to establish a shared space of mutual respect, understanding, and good intent**. You want to communicate that you are good, that they are good, and that you desire for the interaction between you to be good, too. It's an act of benevolent civility and good faith.

Sure, the person you're meeting at that cocktail party is not likely to be from a warring tribe and probably won't threaten to kill you with a spear if you offend them, but your first encounter with them is as important as any that our ancient ancestors would have made way back in our deepest history.

A greeting acknowledges someone's presence. It also *validates* their presence. It sets a frame around the conversation you're about to have. Think of it as drawing a special, temporary circle around your interaction.

Good "manners" are the human equivalent of the non-verbal rituals animals perform when encountering one another in the wild. Etiquette is not some frilly arbitrary thing we invented only recently; it is instead a natural progression from our **earliest instincts for preservation, belonging, survival, and connection.**

Not greeting a friend can cause hurt feelings and misunderstandings because you're not acknowledging their presence. In other words, it will feel like an insult . . . because it is. Neglecting proper greetings is akin to ignoring someone's most basic needs for inclusion and social belonging. Not greeting a stranger carries obvious connotations—you are deliberately choosing not to draw that temporary circle, not to put down your metaphorical "weapons," and not to make any gesture toward knowing them or including them in your social sphere—i.e., letting them remain a potential enemy and outsider.

Proper greetings and introductions can seem inconsequential, but if you get them wrong, they can literally color the rest of your entire relationship with that person. Seems like a pretty big deal when you think about it!

Greetings

There are two types of greetings:

Informal Greetings

Informal greetings can be spoken or gestured. "Hello" and "hi" are classic greetings, while "hey" is popular in some regions. A name and a smile usually accompany the greeting. Some regions hold on to a degree of formality and still say "good morning," "good afternoon," and "good evening." Children and teens have greeting norms of their own, but it's wise not to emulate them since they're usually too informal or else will alienate most people.

Formal Greetings

Sometimes a formal greeting is needed. In business, coworkers may be casual but defer to their boss. In a formal receiving line, even those who know each other well shake hands or exchange social kisses, offer a polite comment, then move on. Formal greetings use "hello" instead of "hi" or "hey." Consider tone and posture. These greetings are usually brief but always friendly and genuine.

Etiquette guides will labor the difference between these two types, but perhaps more important than this is the thing they have in common: **authenticity, presence, and intention**. Whether formal or informal, a greeting should be a deliberate pause and an intentional nod to acknowledge other people. It cannot be rushed or assumed to be unnecessary. It's always necessary. The next time you greet someone, take the time to deliberately pause—even a few seconds is enough—and really immerse yourself in conveying complete warmth for that moment.

This moment of deliberation and presence is the heart of the greeting. If you get this right, every other blunder will likely be forgiven. Keep the following in mind:

- When you rise to greet someone who has just entered the room, you show respect. As a rule, stand whenever you can. This holds true when greeting someone older than you, someone you're meeting for the first time, or someone who is traditionally shown social respect, such as a religious leader or a person of high social rank.
- Always shake hands with eye contact. If you extend your hand and the other person doesn't, assume they didn't see it, drop it, and forget the shake. (Please note that shaking hands is very culturally embedded. Not all cultures follow this tradition, so pause a moment to take a read on what others are doing first if you're unsure).
- Kissing, hugging, and other affectionate gestures can be used to greet your family members or close friends. Be wary of using this kind of greeting for casual acquaintances, as it may cause

discomfort. On the other hand, if someone unexpectedly greets you this way—roll with it!

So, to quickly conclude: a great greeting consists of a deliberate moment of warmth and presence. Smile, acknowledge the other person, and try to convey a genuine feeling of henceforth sharing a mutual space together. **The etiquette rules are there to create a certain *shared emotional experience*—focus on that feeling and it will be far easier to know what to do.**

Introductions

There are many rules about how to introduce people, but the only mistake that can't be made up for is when people who don't know each other don't introduce themselves. Ordering mistakes, misspelled words, and mispronunciations are not as rude as expecting people to be friendly with each other when they don't know who the other people are. If you've ever felt yourself in this cringe-inducing situation, you'll know what a kindness it is for someone to spare you from it!

The goal of the introduction is twofold. First, they help people learn each other's names. Second, they make strangers feel more at ease and comfortable. If you make a mistake, the best thing to do is keep going, smoothing it over with a smile as quickly as you can. Stopping in the middle to fix it and drawing attention to the error will just make everyone confused.

Here are some introduction basics. First, always introduce yourself in new situations, whether it's a chance meeting for a few seconds or a business dinner lasting several hours. When you introduce yourself first, you establish control of the meeting or encounter and demonstrate initiative and an ability to be direct—all plusses in a business situation. Some people feel that an introduction is embarrassing or will come across too forced. The opposite is true, though, and there is far more awkwardness caused later on when you hurry into conversation without one. Without that shared circle being cast, misunderstandings can happen quickly!

Always state your name (clearly!) and offer something about yourself. For example, you might say, "Good morning, Mr. Doe. I'm Harry Smith from Atlas Motors," or, "I'm Kelly. I went to school with your brother!"

In more formal or professional situations, always introduce "from the bottom up." That is, the "lesser authority" is always introduced to the "higher authority" by saying the higher authority's name first. For example, a junior executive should be introduced to a senior executive. Similarly, a company executive should be introduced to a client. This is a small but subtle point that will be registered, even if people aren't sure what they are noticing!

Clients and customers are always considered more important than someone in your firm, even if the client has a lower rank than your colleague. For example: "Ms. Higher Authority, I would like to introduce Mr. Lesser Authority from our legal department. Ms. Higher Authority is the vice president of human resources."

Always highlight the company or position of the individuals you are introducing and, if appropriate, include pertinent information about each. For example, you might say: "Mark Stevens, I'd like to introduce John Doe. He's the senior vice president at ABC Cell Phones and the person to call if you need anything related to cellular phones. John, Mark is president of Stevens Associates, the best PR firm in the country for promoting products." A descriptive introduction eliminates the inevitable silence that often follows as unfamiliar individuals try to guess what the other does or whether they have anything in common. By providing the information, you put each individual at ease and establish an opening for conversation.

The highest-ranking person typically introduces everyone else. The regional manager is introduced to the CEO, then the branch manager, etc. If a client is present, they are introduced first. Always use a person's first and last name and appropriate title when introducing them. Even a close friend of yours shouldn't be introduced to others by first name only. Only children have first names. If you're ever unsure, err on the side of formality and go with second names until being explicitly invited (i.e., don't ask) to use first names.

In less formal situations, consider the context; who is above whom in the hierarchy can be a subtle thing, but pay it some attention. If a child is visiting an as-yet-unmet family member in their home, for example, introduce the child to the family member. If the family member is coming to visit the child in *their* home, however, it may feel more appropriate to introduce the relation to the child. Whether the situation is business or pleasure, formal or not, it's always good etiquette to follow with something that either of the introduced parties can grab hold of so they're not left hanging, trying to think of how to get the conversation going. "This is Jim.

He's also a bit of a film buff, so I'm sure you both will have lots to talk about!"

Finally, always stand for introductions. No exceptions! This goes for both men and women and for both business and social occasions.

Well, let's now consider what *not* to do. Never give yourself an honorific such as "I'm Ms. Doe" or "I'm Dr. Doe" (it's like drinking a toast to oneself), and never assume intimacy just because you've been introduced. When you meet someone for the first time, you should continue to call him or her by his or her title and last name until invited to be on a first-name basis.

Never "meet" people. When introducing people, the proper wording is "Mr. Doe, I'd like to introduce to you Mr. Joe," and not "Mr. Doe, I'd like you to meet Mr. Joe." Try not to respond to an introduction with just "hi" or "hello." When responding to an introduction, you should always repeat the name of the person you are meeting (i.e., "Hello, Mrs. Martin"). Adding a courtesy statement such as, "I've been looking forward to meeting you" is always appreciated.

Smile; focus on that feeling of warmth, rapport, and respect; and take your cues from others if you're   unsure.

Chapter 2: Etiquette in Public

Social etiquette includes all the "little things" we do to avoid big things happening later on! **Any time people interact, there is an opportunity for friction or misunderstanding. Etiquette is the time-tested set of rules that we use to cut this possibility down to a minimum.** You may be surprised to see some of the following etiquette rules in a book on socializing—what do sidewalks and doorways have to do with socializing? But if you've ever had that awkward moment when you bump into someone, stand on their toes, or get into an argument over a bus seat, you know that how we carry ourselves in public spaces is a big part of social interaction!

Sidewalks

Unless you live somewhere rural and always will, you probably will encounter crowds trying to squeeze down narrow sidewalks and pavements. However, if everyone follows a few rules of etiquette and common courtesy, everyone will be able to get where they're going a little bit quicker. Here are some tips to keep in mind:

Tip 1: Stick to your right. Think of the sidewalk like a street. Don't walk into oncoming traffic!

Tip 2: Devices down, eyes up. Looking down to your smartphone is a recipe for disaster and a guaranteed way to make everyone in the street hate you! You could crash into another pedestrian . . . or even worse, a car or bus!

Tip 3: Keep up the pace. Crowded sidewalks typically fall into a sort of default walking speed. Move closer to the buildings to rummage through a bag or answer a text, or you're bound to get bumped! Even better if you can find a little nook, bench, or side street to step into and get out of people's way.

Tip 4: Keep your squad in formation. If you're walking with a big group, spreading out four or five across and taking up the whole sidewalk is bound to annoy and hinder your fellow sidewalk users. If you've been behind such an oblivious crowd before, you'll know how rage-inducing it is!

Doorways

Any time the flow of traffic is restricted, your spidey-senses should alert you to dial up the etiquette and become conscious of those around you.

Tip 1: Let in the person behind you. If a door is getting a lot of traffic, making an effort to prop the door open for the person behind you is a courteous thing to do . . . and it keeps people moving! There's an exception, though. If the person behind you is a long way behind, you may cause more awkwardness holding it while they take another five minutes to get to you, no doubt feeling very self-conscious!

Tip 2: If you're approaching a door that pulls open, pull the door open and allow the person you're walking with to enter first. If you're a gentleman who's been taught to open the door for a lady, feel free to do so, but don't feel like you need to make it into a big, chivalrous display that you immediately expect acknowledgment and praise for. Whatever you do, don't get stuck in a game of "you first, no you first." If the way is offered, graciously and quickly accept and move on.

Tip 3: If you're approaching a door that pushes open, push the door open, entering first, and hold the door open for your companion. Pushing it open and waiting for them to go through might force some uncomfortable physical proximity.

Tip 4: If you encounter someone whose arms are full or who could have some difficulty entering, by all means, say something nice like, "Let me get the door for us."

Tip 5: When meeting someone at work, leave your office or desk and greet the visitor yourself. Show them to your office or meeting room and open the door for them. When the meeting is adjourned, walk your guest to the door and open it for them as they leave. Don't forget to leave after your guests. The same can be done for casual guests to your home.

Tip 6: Never assume that people are comfortable in your home just because you are close friends. Unfamiliar homes will always feel unfamiliar. It's lazy to issue a blanket "me casa es su casa!" and leave them to fend for themselves. Open doors and deliberately invite them to come inside, then show them where you'd like them to walk. The standard "house tour" is not just to show off—it's to help people feel oriented. It's as though you're "introducing" them to the space!

Elevators

Tip 1: When boarding, stand to the right, away from the doors, to allow people to enter behind you.

Tip 2: When an elevator arrives, don't go aboard until all the riders have gotten off (this applies to public transport, too).

Tip 3: If it's not too awkward or inconvenient, hold the door for other riders who are entering. And don't ask a crowded elevator to hold the door as you're approaching. Let them get on their way!

Tip 4: Don't try to squeeze into a crowded elevator with doors closing.

Tip 5: Backpacks down! If you are in a crowded elevator, remove your backpack from your shoulders and hold it close to your legs; it creates space for another person.

Tip 6: If you're standing near the buttons, be willing to push the buttons for people who are farther away if they ask. You might even like to ask—simply raise your eyebrows and ask "floor?" with a smile and that should be enough.

Tip 7: If you're standing in the back of a crowded elevator and your floor is approaching, don't feel bad about saying something like, "Excuse me, my floor is next." That way, people can make room for you to exit.

Tip 8: Exit the elevator to let people going to the floors before yours get out. And then just hop right back in!

Now, we could be here all day if we listed every single physical situation you might find yourself in in a busy metropolis—moving walkways, taxis, park benches, and so on. But you're probably sensing a theme here—**every etiquette rule exists to put other people and yourself at ease and reduce anxiety.** That's it. That means that if you're in a place where there is fast foot traffic, behave in a way that doesn't impede that traffic. If you walk into a place known for its quiet, behave in a way that maintains that quiet. And so on.

Screens and devices are usually seen as impolite purely because they stop people from being cognizant of others—in fact, gazing at a screen in a public place can be seen as incredibly anti-social. If you are always aware of who is around you, however, you can speed up, slow down, or move to get out of the way. Be mindful and considerate. If you're at a baggage claim, for example, don't race ahead and push people out of the way when you see your bag coming down the chute. It's simply a matter of constantly being aware of other people and what they are all assembled in that public space to do.

Common sense is, sadly, not that common, and you are most at risk of breaking unspoken social rules any time you are overly focused on yourself and forgetting that you are actually in a shared space, where other people's needs and intentions matter as much as yours do. This means not running to grab the last seat on the bus when there's an ill and elderly lady behind you. It means keeping phone conversation volumes to a minimum when on busy public transport, and covering your nose when you sneeze in a supermarket.

Most of us feel like we don't need to be *told* not to touch things in a museum or take sexy selfies at a war memorial, but every person making such a faux pas probably never thought of themselves as rude or uncultured! There are dozens upon dozens of etiquette rules for how to behave in public spaces, from the obvious (don't break wind in a restaurant) to the niche obscure (don't say "bravo" if cheering for a single female performer), but all of them come down to a few essential principles:

1. Be aware of others
2. Be aware of yourself
3. Behave in such a way as to make yourself least offensive to others, given the context

Sems pretty simple, right? The trouble is, few of us think of ourselves as rude or inconsiderate people. And to some extent, there's a reason for this: People don't behave this way because they're bad people, but because they are

1. Not aware of themselves
2. Not aware of others
3. . . . which means they can't begin to behave in a way to make themselves least offensive to others

In other words, people break social rules and come across as rude and unlikeable largely *by accident.* If you are distracted, mindless, or too busy stressing about something else, you may be rude without even knowing it.

It's easy to remedy this, though. The next time you enter a public place, literally imagine that there is a switch inside you that turns from "private" to "public." This switch alters the focus of your awareness. When you're at home alone in your own space, your focus is typically turned *inward* toward yourself and your own needs, perceptions, and intentions. But in a public space, you need to change the direction and quality of your focus. You need to be more aware of the context, other people, what they're doing, and especially how they're perceiving you . . . i.e., you need to turn that inner perception *outward*.

Think about two old friends who have just met up after years apart, who are walking down the street having a lively conversation on the way to a coffee shop. They are walking side by side, talking loudly but moving slowly, completely unaware of the aggravated people piling up behind them who don't want to walk that slowly, but who are prevented from overtaking them due to the car traffic on the other side.

Now, these two friends are **not bad people; they're just not paying attention!** They're behaving as though they're in a private world of their own, when in reality, they are in a shared space. In a sense, their lack of awareness is really a lack of *situational empathy*. You can avoid many faux pas like this by simply reminding yourself in public to deliberately make that switch and become more aware of yourself and others and how you are all interacting in that shared space.

Chapter 3: Eye Contact Etiquette

Well, you've behaved yourself in public and made that first greeting and introduction. Now what?

Let's take a closer look at what some would argue is the most fundamental form of communication and the one to master first: eye contact. When eyes meet, two separate gazes come together and two different conscious attentions are momentarily fixed together. With eye contact, it's about so much more than exactly how long you linger on this gaze. Rather, **it's about understanding *contact* (i.e., intimacy) and how to play that up or down depending on the context and your relationship to the person in front of you.**

It's crucial to distinguish between eye contact and staring. Staring is just plain rude and threatening (often done without blinking), but eye contact shows confidence, relaxation, and interest in the other person. It's the difference between gently touching something versus hitting it!

Are you one of those people who finds eye contact extremely awkward? That's totally normal! Try to remember, eye contact equals intimacy. It's powerful stuff, so if you are feeling uncomfortable, you can't go wrong by pulling back and letting your gaze rest elsewhere for a moment. That said, used correctly and deliberately, eye contact can be a good way to gain social mastery and conscious control of any interaction. Here are a few tips.

How much eye contact should you make? Avoid extremes—both 0 percent and 100 percent of the time are going to make a situation awkward fast. Aim for a comfortable 50 percent.

How long should you hold eye contact? Four to five seconds is a good ballpark figure. That said, don't get too hung up on counting in your head! Hold your gaze for the length of one relaxed inhale or exhale and then allow your eyes to look at something else. When you do this, avoid a rapid flitter away and instead slide your eyes easily to the side or down, lest you come across as nervous or overly shy.

When should you make eye contact? There's a reason people say "I see" when they mean "I understand"! In a conversation, try to make eye contact to show that you're listening while the other person is talking. Eye contact while you are speaking can be felt as too forceful if prolonged.

What if it feels really awkward?! Don't worry—try the "triangle technique." First, gaze at the person's eyes for a few moments, then pull away for a moment and look at either their nose or mouth, then return to the eyes after a few seconds. Basically, you imagine a triangle between their two eyes and their nose/mouth, and you flit your gaze between the three points whenever you feel a little awkwardness coming on!

Without a doubt, the unspoken rule with eye contact is that it conveys intimacy, emotion, and interest. That means if you are perceptibly making more eye contact than the other person is, you are basically saying "I'd like to be closer to you," and if you're avoiding eye contact, you are saying "I'd like *less* intimacy, thank you!"

Don't be thrown by the word "intimacy," of course. As we'll see in later chapters, the foundation of all communication is physiological, and *all* communication stems from our more ancient mother tongue, which is body language. So much of our nonverbal communication is based on proximity, contact, and closeness. That means that even before you've said a word, your body has communicated a thousand clear messages to people around you—and eye contact is a big part of this. This is why two people on opposite sides of a massive room can make eye contact and feel "close"!

A Question of Flirting

Speaking of "making eyes," it's worth considering another powerful aspect of eye contact: its flirtation potential. Do you want to know if the person in front of you is romantically interested? Watch their eye contact. **If they gaze at you, then quickly flicker away their glance only to look straight back at you again almost instantly, consider this a sign for "I'm interested."** No, they're not madly in love . . . but you definitely have their attention. If you want to send this message yourself, try to linger on a gaze just a second or two longer than you ordinarily would. You only need to do this once or twice and the other person will *definitely* understand your intention—even if only unconsciously.

That said, think carefully if this is the message you'd like to send to a person you're *not* interested in! Avoid sending the wrong message by keeping your eye contact moving, and mixing up the object of your attention so that you're also looking at other people. In most cultures, a lowered gaze can also suggest flirtation, or possibly the invitation to partake in a shared secret. If this is not what you mean to convey, keep your chin up and facial expression open—this is more associated with friendliness and platonic warmth.

If you are in a strictly platonic or professional relationship, you can instantly strengthen an invisible boundary by immediately breaking off eye contact. Done correctly, this needn't be noticed or uncomfortable; simply pull away eye contact gently to the side and focus on something else. It's an immediate, even subliminal, message that you are dialing back the closeness and intimacy—and it can often avoid embarrassing misunderstandings quickly and clearly, without anyone having to say a word.

Finally, think about cultural aspects. In the US, eye contact is associated with friendliness and trustworthiness. Avoiding it (especially to look downward) can signal submissiveness or lack of self-confidence. If you're very obviously squirming away to avoid eye contact, this is often seen as deceptive—something to bear in mind if you just think of yourself as shy!

However, in certain cultures (for example, many Asian cultures), prolonged direct eye contact can be seen as arrogant, aggressive, rude, or just weird (Uono, Hietanen, 2015). It is considered far more polite to make only fleeting occasional glances and reserve more lingering contact for close friends and family. Averted gazes signal to them respect and tact rather than any kind of weakness. On the other hand, in Muslim cultures, old traditions that limit eye contact between men and women still hold sway.

How are you supposed to know the difference? Well, use your eyes. Look very carefully at what others are doing and mimic them. **This is a communication trick called mirroring, and it will take you far any time you're not sure how to behave**. All you need to do is observe what most people around you are doing and copy them. If everyone is mostly staring at the shared task in front of them, you'll break an unwritten rule by deliberately looking at people's faces while they work. If you're at an intimate family gathering with plenty of warm eye contact, though, and you spend the evening looking into the distance or at your phone, you will be considered rude and disengaged. Again, it's about context and being sensitive to what it requires of you.

Just remember that eye contact is a form of body language. If you match someone else's eye contact, you are signaling rapport and harmony with them; if not, understand that you are nonverbally suggesting that you increase or decrease the level of contact and intimacy between you. Finally, it may seem odd to say, but try not to overthink it too much. If you find yourself feeling anxious and unsure in a conversation, default to no eye contact. Keep smiling, keep breathing, and check in on your body language. Listen closely to what you're being told and try not to be too deliberate. When it comes to eye contact, it's easier to simply make sure you're not doing the wrong thing and then let nature take its course the rest of the way!

Chapter 4: Small Talk Danger Zones

Are you someone who says you "hate small talk?" Time to banish this expression from your vocabulary!

It's a myth that small talk is inconsequential, stupid, boring, unnecessary, or difficult. Actually, it's a myth that there's anything *small* about it at all! Think of small talk as a non-negotiable warm-up—without it, expect the "big talk" to be more fraught with danger and injury than it needs to be!

All of this is to say that a big unspoken rule in any human interaction is that you start small and work your way up. You go for the broad, easy, and simple first and *gradually* work your way to the specific, more challenging, and more complex as you go. Human relationships are built when people increase intimacy, i.e., slowly close the gap between them. But this cannot be rushed. Even two people who are madly in love living happily ever after had to first *start* with a hello and a little chit chat about nothing in particular.

Many people think that small talk is a hindrance, but it's actually what makes it possible to have the deep and meaningful conversations. Why? Because if you barge ahead and try to engage with someone on a very intimate level early on in a conversation, it's a little like rushing up to a stranger and giving them a kiss. It *might* work out for the best . . . but your chances of causing outrageous offense are probably far, far greater! What's more, this offense might be so great that you could permanently put off someone who might have actually wanted to give you a kiss at some point anyway.

That's what small talk is about—lowering the chances of causing offense and increasing the chances of later connection and rapport.

With that in mind, let's look at the topics and ideas that almost all cultures can agree are out of bounds when it comes to successful small talk. Sure, you might talk about these things with people once you know them better. In fact, gradually broaching these topics is a clear signal that you are closing that gap and creating more distance with someone. But unless you're at that point, try to completely avoid the following topics:

1. Appearances
2. Money
3. Sex
4. Politics
5. Religion

Yes, yes, everyone knows that these are the most interesting things! But ignore this rule at your peril. Let's take a closer look.

Appearances

What's the best way to comment on someone's appearance? The answer is: there isn't one. Just don't do it. Period.

Clinical psychologist Dr. Desta suggests the "five second rule," which goes like this:

"You can comment on any aspect of someone's appearance **if and only if they can change it in five seconds.** If it would take them more than five seconds to change it, then hush. Especially if the comment is based on your opinion."

- If someone has a little crumb stuck to the side of their face—you can comment on it since it will only take them a moment to address.
- If someone appears to be tired and disheveled—don't comment, since they can't do much to fix any of that in just five seconds!
- If someone's necklace is on backward—you can say something.
- If someone is dressed too formally for the occasion—stay quiet. There's nothing they can do about it now, right?

Generally, avoid commenting on someone's weight, age, body size, outfit, teeth, scars, acne, injuries, race, hair type or style, height, face structure . . . you get the picture! So if you see someone who's got a horrendous sunburn, keep quiet about it. You saying, "Oh my God, look at your horrendous sun burn!" will only put them on the spot and make them feel uncomfortable and judged.

If you're wondering "what about giving them a nice compliment?" well, this can be as dangerous a minefield as a thinly veiled insult. Consider the topic of weight loss. You see an old friend who's lost a bunch of weight, and say, "Woah, you've lost so much weight. You look amazing!" But later you find out she has been battling cancer and chemo treatment, and her weight loss is something she's deeply embarrassed and unhappy about. Oops. Or perhaps she doesn't have cancer at all and has just naturally lost a bit of weight, but now she thinks to herself, "I didn't think I was fat before . . . but I do now." Oops again—your comment will feel like judgment even if it's intended to be praise.

According to LA eating disorder specialist Dr. Lauren Muhlheim, this is why you should simply avoid commenting on weight, body shape, or eating habits entirely. Even if it feels like you're being complimentary, you are actually making value judgments about what kinds of bodies or lifestyles are better than others. For example, the person being praised for losing weight may register the conditional nature of that statement (i.e., you'll be unhappy if they gain weight), and the other people in the room may wonder, "Does that mean they think badly about *my* body, then?"

It's a minefield. Best to avoid mentioning these topics at all, and that includes things like eating habits—how much you eat, why, what kind of food, when, and so on. This can be just as damaging, if not more so. Avoid commenting on dietary restrictions or things like vegetarianism, on the size of their portion, on how "clean" or healthy their meal is, on the cost, on the way they're eating it, on their appetite, or on their tastes and preferences. Food is a deeply personal matter, and you can quickly cause offense before you know it.

It goes deeper than this, though. **If you want to give a compliment, do so for something you know the person themselves is proud about, i.e., something they can and have controlled.** If you praise someone for their beautiful eye color, you are praising them for something they had no hand in, and therefore it might feel like a completely hollow observation. It's even worse if you compliment them for something that is only valuable to *you* but not them (for example, men may cause offense by complimenting a woman's sexiness, unaware that she regards sexiness as the very least interesting thing about her). People often feel far more validated and seen if you acknowledge their hard work, their strength, their kindness, their unique personality, their creative efforts, or how much dedication they've put into a much-loved project.

Money

This one is much less of a minefield: just don't talk about it!

Appropriate questions and comments:

- A person's job
- What they like about that job
- ... and that's about it

Inappropriate questions and comments:

- Their salary
- How much they have saved or invested
- How much they paid for something, including their house or car
- How much debt they have
- Whether they can afford something or not
- What their credit rating is
- Whether you can borrow money from them!

The reason is obvious—talking about money is a fast track for landing in uncomfortable and awkward territory that may lead to misunderstandings, judgments, and hurt feelings. Don't ask for money advice or give it. Similarly, avoid putting hard figures on things and broadcasting strong opinions about costs. If you say something like, "You'd have to be an idiot to buy that—no coffee machine is worth four thousand dollars," or, "It's only four thousand dollars? What a bargain! I should get two," then you are sending strong, possibly alienating messages to people around you.

If you can, be gracious and avoid overly probing questions, and change the topic if people are being nosy. Money is not just about money, though—try to be mindful and avoid judgments or assumptions about people's backgrounds, their socio-economic class, or what is considered either cheap or a luxury.

Sex, Politics, and Religion

The classic trio . . . and for a good reason!

Steer clear of bringing up these subjects unless you want to run the risk of being thrust into the middle of an, uh, *animated* discussion. All three topics are extremely personal and almost guaranteed to invite disagreement or outright division. It's simply too easy to offend people. And it's never worth it.

If you find this particular conversation rule annoying, just remind yourself that **the function of small talk is not to bring anyone around to your opinion or put the world to rights. It's only about creating connection and rapport**—that's it. It doesn't matter in the least who's "right." Imagine having a relative stranger come up to you and tell you all about exactly what they think of gay adoption, gun ownership, and the good Lord himself. Are you interested? Probably not! Just remember that when you feel compelled to share your opinions with others—in the best way possible, they're likely not interested.

There's nothing to say you can't share all your deepest and potentially controversial opinions with people *later* when you know them better . . . only that there is a time and a place, and it's usually not when you've just met them.

The reason these topics are off-limits is, again, because they create a degree of closeness and intimacy that might not be appropriate or shared. Remember that small talk is *gradual*. It's not merely politeness that keeps you from talking about life after death or feminism or universal basic income with people you don't know well. It's treating more sensitive topics with a greater degree of care and tact.

The Art of Changing the Topic

What do you do if *other* people insist on broaching one of these topics?

Here, some grace and tact are needed, too. **Try some "evasive maneuvers" to change the course of the conversation while**

maintaining friendliness. This can be done by minimally acknowledging the potentially offensive material, then *deciding not to respond to it*, followed by a rapid change of topic.

"Wow, you're so much bigger than when I last saw you!"
"Oh, thank you. You're looking good yourself. So did you have fun at the Halloween party last week?"

"So how much are they paying you for your troubles?"
"Haha, enough! We might be getting a few trainees onboard in the new year, so I'm looking forward to that."

"Anyway, she's dating some kind of creepy right-wing guy now, God help her."
"Oh? I'm sure he's great. What's his name?"

"So that's when my wife asked my girlfriend if she'd mind if my boyfriend's husband came to the sleepover as well, but I told her I hadn't bought enough whipped cream for all of us. You know how it is . . ."
"Oh, of course. Catering for groups can be such a nightmare, right? Anyway, it's been great talking, but I just remembered I need to fetch my dog from the groomers!"

In each case, there's no need to actively respond to something inappropriate, but neither do you have to strenuously flee from it. **Just give it *minimal* acknowledgement, then ignore it and quickly divert with a topic change.**

Even if you do happen to be offended by something someone says, it's almost always worth your while to remain polite and ignore it—after all, taking the bait will only result in unpleasantness, and you're not likely to change any hearts and minds. Indeed, when people disagree in fundamental ways, the most respectful thing to do is acknowledge that it's not a question of who is right or wrong, but rather having the social intelligence to leave contention alone and move on to something you do agree on.

"But I'm Blunt. I Just Call It as I See It."

Have you heard this? Or perhaps *you're* the person saying it?

Well, here's some bluntness: The above sentiment is nothing more than a weak excuse. Choosing not to follow commonly agreed-upon social conventions is not a unique and quirky personality trait. And yes, it is a question of *choosing* to be polite. Those who consider others, adjusting according to context and behaving in ways that promote harmony and connection, are not doing something superhuman or out of the ordinary. And those who forego this effort are not doing so because they are introverts or special somehow or just incapable of doing otherwise.

While that may sound harsh, this attitude is a good one to try to let go of. It serves no one and only reinforces the idea that manners and etiquette are something you're born with, and if it doesn't come naturally, then oh well, it can't be helped! **But *anyone* can learn to become more situationally aware, more respectful, and more tuned into others.** The rules are learned and mastered not solely for other people's sake, but for yours, too. Life will be far more comfortable, easy, and enjoyable.

If you still need convincing, think of the last time someone told you that they were "just sayin'!" or "telling it like it is." How did it feel? Did they come across as authentic, wise, and uniquely able to see through the lies and deceits of everyday niceties? Did you think they were very clever and brave for not following the unspoken rules? Or did you just think they were kind of a jerk?

Summary:

- Good etiquette, manners, and social skills will make you more likeable, a better conversationalist, and more skilled at diffusing conflict. Social skills are natural, but they're not always easy or automatic!
- Prioritize establishing a shared space of mutual respect, understanding, and good intent. Greetings and introductions matter since they speak to people's needs to belong and be included. Never forget to properly greet people. Formally or informally, greet with **authenticity, presence, and intention**.
- Always introduce strangers from the "bottom up" in formal/professional situations.
- Etiquette rules in public are there to minimize friction. Pay attention, minimize device use, and keep out of people's way. Have situational empathy: Be aware of yourself and of others. When in doubt, behave in a way that puts everyone else most at ease.
- Eye contact equals intimacy. Hold contact for four seconds and try the triangle technique to show interest when listening to others speak. Be aware of the power of eye contact to show sexual interest, as well as cultural contexts. If you're ever unsure,

match and mirror other people's eye contact.
- Small talk is an essential part of *gradually* building intimacy. Avoid conversational danger zones: appearances, money, sex, politics, and religion—at least until you know the person better! Gracefully change the topic and keep things moving.
- Finally, don't be the person who is proud to be "blunt"—this is just laziness.

Part 2: The Golden Rule is Respect

Good manners reflect something from inside— an innate sense of consideration for others and respect for self.

–Emily Post

You've navigated the social realm with situational empathy, you've made seamless and comfortable introductions and greetings, and you've begun a little small talk with just enough eye contact to build rapport and gradually, gradually close the distance between you and the person in front of you. Well done! It might not seem like much, but master these small skills and you'll be surprised at just how far-reaching the benefits really are.

Let's move deeper now and consider those situations where you already know someone and must now find a way to negotiate continued interactions with them. Whether in a professional or personal capacity; whether you see them once a year or every day; and whether you want to get to know them better, stay the same, or gently phase them out of your life ... it's worth thinking about etiquette in terms of *respect*.

Chapter 5: Punctuality Is Respect

You've heard that time is money. But time is valuable in other ways. Most things in life can be negotiated to some degree, but the resource we call time is fixed: We all only have a limited amount of it, and once it's gone, it's gone, and nothing anybody can ever do will bring it back. Time is like gold—its value holds, and it is a perfect standard against which to compare many other values. This is why we'll start with an unspoken etiquette rule that tells us that punctuality is respect—that is, it is respect for someone else's time.

When we pay attention to avoiding small talk danger zones, when we give people space to walk on the sidewalk, and when we are careful and conscientious with our eye contact, we are respecting people's lives and their personal space. **When we are punctual and time efficient, we are respecting their time limitations.**

By doing this, you build up your reputation for being a person who is honest, trustworthy, and respectful. The crucial thing about this kind of reputation, though, is that it's not about what you say, but what you do. Your character is made up of each and every little action you take—including the actions you *don't* take. That means that it's not enough to simply mean well and have good intentions, and it's not enough to just claim that you're a respectful person.

When you are on time, you are not just communicating respect for the other person, but showing respect for yourself, too. You demonstrate that you are in command of the situation, that you are conscious and aware, and that you are able to plan and prioritize. You show others that you value your own time and don't intend to waste it, either! It's no surprise, then, that punctuality features so heavily in lists of etiquette rules.

It's about planning and foresight. If you have many tasks to do in a day, and some of them are time sensitive, take a moment to plan *well before* you need to do them or get ready. It only takes a few minutes to look at your to-do list for the day and predict how long each task will take and which ones are most important.

Once you've identified all your time obligations for the day, you need to be realistic—very realistic! People who struggle with time management usually have a special kind of optimism in that they always think things will be achieved in much less time than they realistically will. If you know that your dental appointment will take an hour, for example, and that it takes ten minutes to drive there and back, factor in a little extra time—assume it will take ten minutes more at the dentist and five minutes more each way. It might feel like this is wasting time, but you'll be surprised how often those extra few minutes come in handy. Traffic, unexpected delays, and getting lost can all demolish the most carefully planned schedule. If you have many little "cushions" planned all throughout the day, however, one delay doesn't threaten to ripple through every other appointment.

Here's another trick. Let's say you are at the dentist, but it's important that after an hour you leave and get home so you can make an important Zoom call for work. Knowing this, you ask the dentist *before* you even start the appointment how long she anticipates it will take. If you know ahead of time that you have an upcoming schedule crunch, you can choose there and then to cancel your dental appointment or phone ahead and reschedule the Zoom call. Either way, a single moment of preparation can save you the stress and embarrassment of rushing and leaving people waiting.

Nobody can prepare for unforeseen situations, and you are not being rude by having an emergency or delay that's out of your hands. **But even when you have no control over the situation, you still have the option to consider others and let them know you'll be late**. Let's say you chat with the dentist and realize you won't make your Zoom call after all. However, since you won't get another dental appointment soon, you ask for five minutes to quickly let work know that you're going to be running a little late, or else ask if it would be easier to reschedule entirely. Yes, it's a little awkward and seldom convenient for other people—but it's far better than standing people up or being late!

Even if the situation is difficult and awkward because you have to cancel, you will still maintain your reputation and keep things respectful by keeping people in the loop and taking responsibility. The worst thing you can do is be careless with other people's time . . . and then not be accountable for it. While most people will tolerate five minutes' tardiness here and there, if you are even a minute late, apologize and own up to it—that means no blaming something or someone else!

Are you someone who is always late fifteen minutes or more to everything? Congratulations—you're a person who's always on time. You just need to shift that time up fifteen minutes! Wake up fifteen minutes earlier, leave the house fifteen minutes earlier than you need to, and deliberately plan to arrive fifteen minutes before everyone else. The world is full of clocks, alarms, and apps to help you manage time. **All it takes is awareness of what you're doing and willingness to work on your organization for another's benefit.**

In the morning, set two or even three alarms and put them somewhere that you'll have to get up to turn them off. Set smaller alarms, too, to help you keep track of your progress getting ready in the morning. For example, have the alarm beep when it's time to stop breakfast and start getting showered and dressed, then another one alerting you when it's time to start making your way out the door. Sometimes, people wake up an hour earlier but end up thinking, "Oh, I have plenty of time!" and then get stuck dawdling on one task so that they're still late in the end. Having little alarms as signposts along the way will help you keep track.

Finally, what about when other people are not on time? Well, you're allowed to be unhappy about it, but remain polite. A few minutes late is seldom a big deal, unless it's an ultra-important event (like your own wedding, for example). Be gracious and forgive occasional slip-ups but realize that you are under no obligation to accommodate a person's lateness, either. If they are fifteen minutes late for an hour appointment, end the time you planned to, especially if it means honoring other commitments. In other words, **never allow another person's tardiness to become *your* tardiness.**

... And So Is Keeping Your Word

One obvious reason that being on time is polite and respectful is it is evidence that you are someone who does what they say they will. You can be counted on. Sure, it's only a small thing, but over time it comes to reflect your overall character and trustworthiness.

Why do people not follow through on the things they promise to do? They're not bad or impolite—rather, it's their **misguided desire to please that often makes them over-**

promise and under-deliver. For example, you've started a new job and you're desperate to make a good impression, so when your boss asks you to do a difficult task, you immediately say yes without really considering if you're able to do it. All you know is that you want to appear capable and enthusiastic. And, when you say what you think they want to hear, you *do* appear that way.

That is, until it becomes obvious that you actually cannot follow through. Most of us have been taught since childhood that it's bad to break promises, but many of us still do it all the time in smaller, subtler ways. We might build up other people's expectations because we want to overinflate our skill or come across as more than what we really are. We announce all the things we intend to do because we think it's what people want—but actually what they really want is for us to *do* it!

Merriam-Webster's definition of a promise is: "a statement that one will do or not do something specified; or a legally binding statement that gives the person to whom it is made the right to expect or demand the performance or forbearance of a specified act."

When we make a promise, we are telling someone else that they can count on us and expect certain behavior from us. It's not unlike telling them that we'll meet them at noon—we are asking them to trust that we will indeed behave this way. **Because people take a small risk every time they choose to believe in our promises, it damages trust in a big way when that promise is broken.** In time, people will not be interested in hearing your promises and will simply assume that you can't be trusted and to take everything you say with a pinch of salt.

A small broken promise does damage too. In fact, many smaller cracks in a building can tumble it just as surely as one big one can. It might not always feel like it in the moment, but it's always better to set realistic expectations and then follow through instead of promise big but never keep your word.

Not keeping your promise to others actually has another, unappreciated consequence: You lose faith in *yourself*. If you know that you don't do as you say you will, then why would you believe yourself when you make a New Year's resolution? The tricky thing about having a bad reputation is that you also have a bad reputation with *yourself*. That's not all that different from low self-confidence.

How do you become one of those people whose "word is their bond"?

Tip 1: Don't make promises! It sounds glib, but only make a promise when you're super sure of being able to follow through. Any small disappointments in the present are easier to deal with than big disappointments later.

Tip 2: Have rock-solid boundaries. Know yourself and what you're capable of, know your limits, and be realistic. Don't allow others to coax a promise out of you. Say no to things you don't actually want to do with assertiveness and confidence. Think carefully before agreeing to something (more on this later).

Tip 3: Take your time. There's no rule you have to respond to any requests immediately. Ask for some time to think things through ("let me check my calendar and get back to you") and then you won't walk into something you can't get out of later.

Tip 4: Be clear and specific. You might break a promise simply because you misunderstood what was expected of you, or the time frame in which people thought you'd act. Don't make assumptions. You might say, "I'll help you plan your party. You can count on me," but you didn't realize just how much work the other person thought you were signing yourself up for.

Tip 5: Communicate early. Just like lateness, the sooner you can convey that you can't follow through, the better. Ideally, you would not agree to something you couldn't do. But if you make a promise and quickly discover it can't be done, communicate that as soon as you possibly can.

Tip 6: If you must break a promise, do it well. We'll consider the art of making apologies a little later in the book, but if you have already broken a promise, there's still a chance to redeem some of your reputation in how you handle it. Sometimes, people are forced to break promises through no fault of their own. If this is the case for you, you can actually turn it to your advantage. Take responsibility anyway, then immediately offer an apology and an alternative to help put things right. You might be able to deliver halfway on the promise or do it a little later than originally agreed. What matters is your attitude of wanting to reconcile and find rapport again.

One word of warning, though: if you've broken a promise, be very wary of jumping right in and making another one in a bid to say sorry. It will feel like a demand on the other person, and you will potentially set yourself up for an even bigger letdown later on. Instead, **focus on what you can do here and now to improve the situation.** People almost always value concrete action that makes things better right now, than promises for something grand and lofty in the future.

Chapter 6: The Power of Respecting Other's Opinions

Today, it's fashionable to talk about compassion, kindness, and empathy. The truth is, most of us are not even halfway to being genuinely kind and compassionate to one another and have yet to master the simpler challenge of civility, respect, and basic courteousness. Sadly, our world encourages and emphasizes divisions. We treat our own opinions as sacred and take as a human right our entitlement to not have to deal with people who hold different ones.

We speak about "tolerance" as though it's something we grant others as a gift from our throne as the reigning Good Guy who just always happens to be right all the time. We say "you do you" and claim that people have a right to their opinions, but how many of us *genuinely* believe that? How many of us behave as though that were true?

This is one area in which old-school etiquette might have the most to teach us. The big insight here is that **respecting someone else's perspective literally costs us nothing**—it does not mean we respect ourselves any less or believe in our opinion any less or are threatened in any way. It simply means that we maturely acknowledge that other people are not the same as us and have the right to look at the world in a different way.

Everyone has their own unique set of life experiences that prompt them to think and perceive things in a certain way—after all, this is exactly how you came to possess *your* unique worldview, isn't it? Truly polite, respectful, and mature people understand that it isn't a chore to try to appreciate difference—they may actively enjoy that the world is not filled with people identical to themselves!

You don't have to agree with them or "concede defeat" or behave as though you're being attacked. Try it next time you encounter someone who doesn't agree with you. What does it feel like to just . . . allow them to do that? You'll probably notice that it's a relief not to instantly feel compelled to respond, argue, evaluate, judge, defend, and so on. This can be a big revelation: **All arguments and disagreements are optional.** Do you *want* to have conflict with someone, or would you rather have an interesting conversation with them in which you may even learn something?

Back in the day, people were told, "If you can't find something nice to say, then don't say anything." It sounds trite, but there's wisdom there. You don't *have to* argue with a person, judge them, goad them on, or be rude. Supremely gracious and self-possessed people have a way of rising above all that. Think of two dignified statesmen whose countries are literally at war . . . it doesn't mean they can't sit politely at a table and drink tea and appreciate a good tête-à-tête. They are self-possessed, non-reactive, and good humored. You can be that way too, and it starts with simply being aware that conflict is always a *choice*. You can't help that people are different and may disagree, but you have a lot of control over *how* you disagree.

Many people are reluctant to respect others because they feel that they lose something in doing so—in fact, the opposite is true. When you conduct yourself with respect, you cover yourself in an aura that invites other people to treat you with the same consideration and graciousness. Take a look at some of these everyday examples.

Someone you're talking to suddenly expresses the view that most men will eventually be unfaithful, and the ones who appear to be honest are just the ones who haven't been caught yet. You find yourself taken aback by this—not least because you're a man yourself! You feel your hackles rising, and you instantly want to hit back and point out the obvious flaws in such a mean and sweeping generalization. But you don't. Instead, you ask questions. "Wow, that's interesting. Why do you feel that way?"

It's not just the words you're saying, though—you genuinely want to understand more and to convey a sense of respectful curiosity to the other person. Notice how when you focus on them, your opinion is no longer front and center. Be secure in your own perceptions to know that you don't need to forcefully defend or explain yourself.

After a little civil conversation, and after you politely explain your perspective, the conversation might take some interesting turns. You may find that you're able to see their perspective much better when they explain why they arrived at the conclusion they did.

And, if you carry yourself with respect, you may be surprised at how ready other people are to acquiesce to your point of view, too.

Even if after a few minutes you discover the person is angry, resentful, and not being fair in their argument, there's still no problem at all. You simply say, "Well, I can't say I agree with you there!" and you move on. You see, disagreement—even strong disagreement—doesn't *have* to be a reason to go nuclear, terminate a friendship, or engage in battle till a single winner is declared.

Here's another example. Let's say someone is saying something inflammatory about welfare fraud. It's an emotional topic, certainly, but there's a very simple way to quell that controversial fire and bring things under control: with boring, objective facts. This is not to say you become that annoying know-it-all who thinks that science and "logic" will resolve every issue, but rather that you stay close to what *everyone* can objectively agree is true.

Any time you find a conversation veering off into contentious territory, see if you can pause and backtrack to the last point on which everyone actually did agree. Think of it as a conversational "save point." Alternatively, you might have to introduce such a fact and emphasize everyone's mutual agreement with it. This brings in some calm and takes away opportunities for misunderstandings and hurt feelings. It also neutralizes things and makes them about the *topic*, not about the *person* talking about the topic. Sometimes, you may only be able to find the narrowest common ground—that's okay. **Remember that a disagreement doesn't compel anyone to go into war mode to hash it out**. Just peacefully allow the disagreement to be what it is.

A few things to be on guard against (and it's very easy to do all of these!):

- Forget the word "wrong" at all. People are not automatically incorrect just because they disagree with you, and you'll invite friction if you tell them they're wrong. The same goes for calling people "irrational." Life's contentious issues are too big to be broken down into right and wrong camps, in any case.
- Don't pretend to listen—actually listen. You won't win any hearts by acting as though you're broad-minded. You actually have to be!
- Avoid the dreaded "I'm just playing devil's advocate . . ."

- Don't fear conflict or disagreement, because honest conflict has more value than dishonest harmony does.
- Don't express shock or surprise at someone's view, or suggest in any way that they are crazy, unintelligent, bad, embarrassing, or uninformed to believe such a thing. Intellectual snobbery is often just veiled laziness. The next time you discover someone outside of your ordinary bubble, get excited—you have a chance to genuinely grow and understand more about the world.
- Avoid continually laboring the point and trying to get people to see things as you do. They probably *do* understand where you're coming from, they just don't agree. It's not your job to change their mind!
- Don't talk to a strawman. Real people and their views are often far more subtle and complex than we give them credit for. Ask questions. Assume that the person in front of you is *not* an idiot and that they've come by their opinion honestly. Assume their position makes sense and is rational and internally consistent. Then go from there.

Too many people think that intolerance and narrow-mindedness are somehow problems that only *other* people have—never themselves. They believe that they are open and accepting, but what they really mean is "I'm open and accepting . . . of those people who already agree with me." They may have a special category of people in their minds who they believe don't actually count—*these* people, they unconsciously think, don't really *deserve* respect because they're the bad guys! Can you relate? They may say, "Well, I'm a live-and-let-live kind of person . . . except *them*? Well, that's different . . ." Fairness, self-control, and a generosity of spirit require us to respect *everyone's* views—yes, even that special category of people you're thinking about right now!

Finally, there's a kind of disrespect that is a little less well known but just as damaging: The **disrespect that comes whenever we automatically assume that other people's views are identical to our own.** We might behave or speak as though they are just like us and have our same values. This is disrespectful on a very fundamental level because it tells the other person we have not fully acknowledged or accommodated their individuality and their separateness from us. It tells other people that we are so arrogant, we just assume that our perspective is *the* perspective.

Have you ever had the experience of suddenly discovering a surprising unknown aspect to someone you thought you knew? Maybe you discovered they had radically different politics or religion to you, that they're secretly much richer or poorer than you, or that they have completely different philosophies about life. The point is, even with those we appear to have much in common with, we can continually be surprised at the richness and variety of personal belief. People are not stereotypes—they're unique, colorful, and sometimes contradictory. All the more reason to not delve into sex, politics, and religion right off the bat!

How to Disagree Gracefully

Differences of opinion are not a problem. The way we respond to these differences is what ultimately counts.

Try to hear and reflect the emotional core of what you're told and listen for universal truths.

Let's say someone tells you they believe that it's acceptable—desirable, even—to punish children physically with spanking, etc., whereas you're horrified by the idea and believe it basically amounts to child abuse. But instead of leading with your disagreement, find a way to *lead with agreement.* For example, "I agree with you that it's a parent's duty to take their child's discipline seriously, and I can definitely see that in the end we both care about making sure that children grow up as happy and well-adjusted as possible..."

Importantly, you don't need to qualify this position with "but" (which only cancels out what you've just said!). Just listen closely for the emotional and universal truth in what you're hearing. Yes, even the most outrageous opinion has a kernel of truth to it!

Try to validate their opinion, despite disagreement.

You disagree, but that doesn't mean that they are wrong, stupid, or bad. Validating someone's position simply means we acknowledge that it makes sense, in exactly the same way that our opinions make sense to us. Literally say, "that makes sense" or "I can see why you think that" and you will communicate a respectful acknowledgement of that person's perspective without claiming it as your own or denouncing it.

"I know that you take your job as a parent very seriously, so I'm sure you've given this a lot of thought. I hear what you say about young children not having well developed self-control and how you need to set hard limits. I suppose it is logical, then, that you would believe it's worth using physical punishment..."

Try to resist the desire to come to conclusions.

In disagreements it can sometimes feel like someone needs to win or convince the other, and that this battle needs to be concluded there and then. But it's very seldom the case that consensus is required, and if it is, it's seldom required immediately. State your opinion comfortably, but don't be afraid to contextualize it and put caveats on it: "I can't say I agree with you there, but I'm willing to be proven wrong" or "I can't get on board with that entirely, but I might change my mind if I knew a bit more about it." This is assertive yet keeps the door open.

"I've heard a lot about the damage that spanking can do to children psychologically, but if I'm honest, I haven't really looked for research done to support its benefits. I'm willing to update my view if the research proves me wrong!"

Chapter 7: Respecting Personal Space

In a way, we have already discussed in previous chapters the concept of respecting space: When we are cognizant of eye contact and the "closeness" it implies and when we respect people in public and shared spaces, we are dealing with the core of etiquette—mutual acknowledgment of and respect for personal space. You might think that this simply refers to the literal amount of space we leave empty around one another, but really, **there are strong connections between *psychological space* and physical proximity.** How close we hold our bodies in space is just a reflection of how close we are, metaphorically speaking!

Think of your personal space as the air between your body and an invisible shield or bubble you've made around yourself. The distance between you and your shield probably changes from person to person, depending on things like:

- how well you know the other person
- the kind of relationship you have with them
- how much you trust them
- what you are currently trying to communicate
- your culture and upbringing
- whether you live in a crowded or sparsely populated area
- the immediate social context and environment

Being aware of personal space means you can use it as a factor in communication. In fact, this is the premise of "proxemics." In the 1960s, anthropologist Edward Hall came up with the word "proxemic zone" and divided it into four main categories: the intimate space, the personal space, the social space, and the public space (Hall et al., 1968).

The point is to be aware of what zone interactions are taking place in, as well as to learn how you can navigate changes from one zone to another, and what those changes might signal. Often, a breach in unspoken social rules or an etiquette violation is the result or cause of one or both parties making an unwanted change in proxemic zone. Let's look at some examples.

As a general rule, **the closer the relationship, the smaller the distance**.

In the US, the average comfort levels of personal space look like this:

- Around zero to twenty inches for intimate couples (intimate space)
- Around one and a half to three feet for good friends and family members (personal space)
- Approximately three to ten feet for casual acquaintances and coworkers (social space)
- More than four feet for strangers (public space)

Of course, this differs between cultures. Latin Americans and Middle Eastern cultures tend to be comfortable with smaller distances, whereas East Asian societies and North Americans tend to prefer a little more room. Likewise, city dwellers tend to tolerate far more proximity (think about standing in queues or being on public transport) than rural folks (who might be used to being the only person for miles!). Finally, there are unspoken rules about the optimal proximity between men and women, and parents and children. For example, Middle Easterners may be more comfortable than average with tactile affection between friends, but only provided the friends are of the same sex. Between men and women, their preferred social distance is *greater* than average.

The Intimate Zone

The intimate zone is the space occupied by lovers, family members, and very close friends. It's also the space where contact sports occur, as well as things like massages and health care, and even physical violence!

This is naturally the most intimate zone and signals the greatest degree of trust, liking, and familiarity. However, the small distance is an *effect* of the degree of intimacy in a relationship, not a *cause*. That means that if you get into this zone with someone who doesn't like, know, or trust you, you risk offense and awkwardness. In fact, the intimate zone is the region with the chance for the highest offense to be caused.

So what are the unspoken etiquette laws of the intimate zone? Stay out of the intimate zone if:

- You are not actually on intimate terms with that person!

- You are in a social situation where it is not appropriate (for example, no groping in a church)
- The other person is close to you but currently not interested in intimacy (for example, your girlfriend is busy or presently unhappy with you)

There are a few other rules, too. For men at urinals, the rule is that you can stand close (physical proximity) out of necessity, but avoid psychological proximity by staring straight ahead and avoiding conversation. Likewise, someone might be forced into proximity with you (for example, at a crowded stadium, on a busy train, or because they're a nurse doing a physical exam), but this doesn't imply psychological proximity. In situations like this, lower perceived proximity by avoiding eye contact, orienting the body away from the other person, and keeping dialogue to a minimum.

If you're in a flirty situation where you deliberately intend to *build* more intimacy, then your job is to *gradually* close that distance . . . emphasis on gradually! Invade personal space all at once and you will come across as rude, awkward, or even threatening. Instead, take a small step closer, *then pause and observe.* Watch to see how the other person reacts. If they comfortably maintain the new, smaller distance or even move closer themselves, great! They are happy and comfortable ramping up intimacy. If they pull back or turn away, consider it a clear sign that, at least for the time being, they are not interested in escalating intimacy.

The Personal Zone

Personal space is usually between one and four feet and is the zone people occupy when they are being friendly and congenial.

At this distance, you are no longer a stranger in the background, but your position alone communicates that an interaction of some kind is underway. The unspoken rule is that women generally have smaller social distances than men. Whether this is because they choose to do so or because they've been socialized to take up less room and be more accommodating to proximal intrusions is a fascinating question. Whatever the reason, it's worth always being mindful of the obvious extra dimension introduced between men and women. As a rule, to avoid offense or misunderstanding, men should err on the side of caution and close proximal distance with a woman only when clearly invited to do so.

If you are getting to know someone, be aware that leaning in and having a closer distance may make you appear warmer and friendlier. Many people are confused when they adopt all the correct body language rules and are still perceived as cold and aloof—it's usually because they're standing too far away!

Personal space can be increased or decreased as a way to communicate. For example, during a conversation where you want to foster feelings of friendliness, you might dramatically lean in, lower your voice, and touch the person's forearm as you share a funny and embarrassing story about yourself. All together, these things communicate an obvious message: "I'm welcoming you into my personal space and inviting you to trust me and be my friend." This moment of closeness can be extremely brief, yet the message is communicated loud and clear.

The Social Zone
An easy way to imagine the size of the social zone is to picture yourself walking down the street, and then imagine that you ask someone for the time. The distance you stand at is the social zone—anywhere from three to ten feet.

At this range, you are interacting but on a more detached level. Formal business is

conducted in this zone, as is any interaction with someone you've just met or are encountering in a social event where it is not just the two of you. It's a safe, neutral zone where you can exchange information and pleasantries without necessarily being friendly or close. But it's also a zone where manners and social convention become important. This is the distance in which you make introductions and greetings, and it's the distance you stay at when interacting with service people or colleagues.

As a rule, come out of this zone only if there is a definite signal to make things more personal and intimate. For example, at work, you and your friend maintain a professional distance, but after hours you are happy sitting closely together in a cab on the way to a bar, where you also lean in close as you chat. The change in distance signals that you are now in friend mode rather than colleague mode!

The Public Zone
This distance is four to twenty-five feet . . . or beyond. Greater distances come into play when you're addressing a crowd—the bigger the crowd, the greater the distance usually required. **It's the realm of strangers** and people passing one another in airports, streets, and shopping malls. *The rule is no contact—* **either eye contact or physical contact—and**

no conversation. Here, the public etiquette rules for elevators, doorways, etc. discussed earlier come into play. You can probably see now that these unspoken rules are designed to ease awkwardness between people who are in the public zone but must temporarily be closer than they'd like.

So how do we actually use these insights from proxemics in daily interactions? Keep a few basic rules in mind: Remember that **proximity equals intimacy, and if you change the proxemic zone, you are communicating a change in degree of intimacy**. Another golden rule is to err on the side of greater distance until you are certain that closing that distance is welcome, appropriate, and something you actually wish to communicate at that time. When social rules are broken, they're typically broken because people were *too close*, not too far. A few more unspoken rules you might break without realizing it:

- It is generally acceptable to be closer to children than adults, but unless absolutely necessary, completely avoid touching children you don't know. It was used to engage with and even discipline children you didn't know, but today it is more acceptable to grant children the same personal space as you would an

adult. This means no demanding or forcing a hug or kiss no matter who you are!
- Unless you're already on intimate terms, do not casually touch people's hair, faces, or clothing.
- If there is a large public space, make sure that you distribute yourself evenly with others throughout that space. In other words, if there are one hundred seats and all but one of them are empty, it's a huge faux pas to seat yourself directly beside the only person sitting there.
- Don't read over people's shoulders, look at their phone screens, or peer inside their purses or bags.

The next time you're in a social situation, zoom out for a moment and see if you can look at the scene as an alien from outer space would. Ignore the words being spoken and look only at the most basic messages being communicated by proximity alone. For example, someone might be *saying*, "Oh, that's so interesting," but as they do so, they're leaning far back and angling their body away from the speaker. In this case, **assume that the message communicated nonverbally is the more truthful one!**

Chapter 8: Having Respect for Boundaries

Nowhere is the overlap between psychological and proximal space more obvious than when we talk about boundaries. However, when it comes to personal boundaries, they're just that—personal. It is always our duty to respect other people's boundaries. It is not our job to decide where those boundaries are on their behalf, or to decide whether we agree with them. It is not for us to see if their boundaries make sense or match ours. It is not ever appropriate to negotiate with someone who has stated a boundary, or see how we can maneuver around it. **The unspoken social rule (one that is sadly broken all the time) is that you respect someone's boundary, no exceptions, no questions asked.**

That said, a boundary is never a demand—it is merely giving people the space they need to be themselves. If we walk up to a stranger and punch them in the nose, we've clearly crossed a boundary. But boundary violations can be far more subtle and complicated than this. Consider the following examples:

- Person A tells Person B they are busy, but Person B begs and pleads for their help anyway, asking again and again when Person A says they can't help. When Person A finally caves, Person B praises them for being a good friend.
- A husband goes into his wife's handbag to borrow a few coins for the parking machine.
- A sister barges into her brother's room without knocking first, and then when he protests, she teases him about what he has to hide.
- A wife interrupts her husband to explain to his friend what he "really means."
- A physiotherapist asks prying questions about his patient's sex life, then offers advice.
- A mother borrows her daughter's clothing and invites herself along to meetups with her friends.

Any time we intrude on a person's physical body or personal space, encroach on their resources (including money, time, material things), make unrealistic demands, use guilt and shame to get our way, ignore the word "no," or rush in to insert our own opinion, perspective, or need in a shared situation, we are breaking a boundary. Again, this comes down to a question of respect and being aware that other people, *because they're other people*, may have boundaries and limits that we don't necessarily understand, agree with, or share.

Nobody likes to think of themselves as a boundary-breaker, but we can inadvertently do just that even (and especially) when we think we are helping. Whenever we feel we know best or that we wish to impose our perspective on a situation, we are violating others even if only in small ways. Just as people are entitled to their own private bubble of personal space around their bodies, imagine that they are also entitled to psychological, mental, emotional, and perceptual boundaries, too. Imagine that each person lives in their own little world (just like you) and harmonious communication depends on us recognizing this fact.

Visualize one friend has another friend over for dinner. One friend, keen to make a good impression and fulfill their need to be a good host, continually offers the other one food. The visitor declines again and again, and the host joyfully dismisses this and continues to offer food, drink, desserts. On the tenth offer, the visitor explains that they are trying to watch their weight, and the host immediately launches into several compliments about the visitor's figure and how silly they are to worry about dieting and what their personal philosophy on life and eating is, as well as their own weight and plenty of details about their bowel movements.

As you can see, there are about five hundred boundary violations here! But again, we see they do not come from malice. Good intentions, however, are not enough. **We need to understand what the other person is comfortable with, not what WE are comfortable with or what we think they should be comfortable with.** In other words, if the visitor says, "No cake for me, thank you," then a good host smiles, nods, and does not ask them several dozen more times! This is not dissimilar from polite disagreement. Even though *the host* thinks cake is marvelous and that moderation is better than abstinence, they have the tact to recognize that this is not how it is for their visitor. Instead of essentially denying the visitor's perceptions and limitations, the host dismisses them and continually tries to substitute their own perspective and system of meaning. This dynamic will be familiar to you if you've ever left a friendly and happy family event mysteriously feeling like you've been beaten up—in a way, you have!

Instead, trust people to know their own limits. **Acknowledge that they have the right to set their own terms for their own lives whether it makes sense to you or not.** Especially grant them the right to do so when it would be more convenient and comfortable for *you* if they were more compliant! If you can genuinely accomplish this, you will quickly earn a reputation for trustworthiness and kindness, and a pleasant side effect is that people will be far more ready to respect *your* boundaries when you assert them.

When people think of asserting boundaries, they typically think of uncomfortable situations that are actually quite far advanced. But etiquette, manners, and a little mindfulness exist to actually help you avoid these potential conflicts long *before* they become this awkward. This highlights an important principle: a little firmness, clarity, and respect early on saves everyone from conflict and unpleasantness later on. Think of the person who, wanting to be "polite," agrees to go on a date with someone they don't actually like. Then they agree to another. On the third date, the situation has become so strained, they have to be outright *rude* to bring things to an end, and the other person (maybe rightly) accuses them of leading them on. In hindsight, you've probably learned yourself that it's always much less awkward and uncomfortable to quickly assert a boundary long before it is breached than to have to violently assert it once it's already been transgressed.

In that spirit, here are the unspoken rules for both respecting and defending a boundary (you'll notice that it's basically the same skill set!).

How to Respect Other People's Boundaries

Tip 1: Don't make people repeat themselves. If someone is timid, unsure, or not very assertive, that doesn't mean they are any less entitled to assert their boundary. It isn't an invitation to negotiate or push on the boundary. Basically, no is no. There's seldom any need to ask if people are sure or to try to find some wiggle room. You'll communicate respect and dignity for you both if you take people's word for it and move on.

Tip 2: Don't punish people for their boundaries. This is definitely creeping into abusive territory, but it's something almost all of us are guilty of to some degree. It's manipulation, pure and simple. If someone tells you they can't come to your party, don't say it's fine, only to follow that with a sarcastic dig about how you understand that everything else is more important to them than you are. Responding to people's limits with passive aggression, judgment, suspicion, or hurt is not actually respecting their boundaries. You're just saying, "I'll be respectful . . . but it'll cost you!" This may damage trust even more than outright violating a boundary.

Even if you do feel upset or disappointed because they cannot fulfill a request, for example, understand that that is about *you*—your feelings about their boundaries are not their problem, and they are not compelled to act in ways to offset that or "make it up to you" some other way. Feeling rejected, embarrassed, surprised, angry, sad, etc. are all valid feelings, but they're something to process on your own time. Just because your response is valid, it doesn't mean that their boundary isn't.

Tip 3: Nonverbal cues count, too. Remember the person who was saying "that's interesting" but forcefully leaning back to get away from the other person? In some situations, you may need to be alert and mindful to the fact that people may not always communicate their boundaries clearly and verbally. Women especially may be socialized to always be kind, sweet, and accommodating. This makes it very difficult for them to firmly say no, so they may end up sending confusing mixed messages. In this case, if you do notice that someone's nonverbal communication doesn't match their verbal communication, assume that you are making the person uncomfortable, and err on the side of retracting demands and taking a step back, physically or figuratively.

Tip 4: Be open-minded and understand that things can change. People are complex. Their boundaries depend on their wants and limits, and these things will change over time. Recognize that people are allowed to change their mind about what is comfortable for them. People are not beholden to a boundary for the rest of time. This is why communication is important—because limits are boundaries that are constantly moving, they need to be communicated more than once.

Tip 5: Forgive yourself if you don't always get it right. Even with the best of intentions, mistakes happen and misunderstandings can hurt feelings. Everyone will accidentally violate a boundary now and then—we're only human. See what you can learn from the situation and move on; beating yourself up about it helps nobody.

How to Respectfully Assert Your Own Boundaries

Guess what? All the respect and dignity that you are responsible for giving others is something that you yourself are also entitled to! Boundaries are two-way things, and you are perfectly within your rights to know your limits, communicate them, and take action if others don't respect them. But though you are entitled to your own limits, it is your job to communicate them and assert them.

Tip 1: Communicate clearly, early, and often. People cannot read your mind. Don't assume that *anything* is obvious. If you don't like something, say so. Don't wait for others to guess how you feel and then get angry when they guess wrong. Also, it's a good idea to be proactive and speak up before the situation comes to a head. This could be as simple as stating at the start of a meeting that you only have an hour and have to tend to other commitments after that hour. The earlier you establish what your boundary is, the more casual and relaxed you can be, and the easier it is to carry yourself with confidence and dignity. People who have trouble asserting boundaries often think that it's awkward or will alienate other people—in fact, others are often relieved and put at ease if you are clear, calm, and friendly. That's because they know exactly where they stand with you.

Tip 2: Do not apologize, explain, or justify. You are entitled to have a boundary just because you are a human being. You never have to present a boundary to someone as though you are making an argument that you hope they will like or agree with. Being polite is one thing, but you don't have to walk on eggshells or try to offer them something else to soften your rejection or denial. Finally, when you apologize, you are actually weakening your assertion, not strengthening it. You are never the bad guy for saying no, and the other person's feelings are their responsibility, not yours. If you are worried you'll feel guilty for saying no, try to gain some distance. Ask for a little time after a request, or respond to it in writing so you have more control.

Tip 3: Take your own boundary seriously. Too many people set a boundary, assert it . . . and then do precisely nothing when people trample over it again and again. It's important to understand that setting a boundary isn't making a claim about how others should behave—it's a claim on how *you* will behave. It's saying "these are the conditions under which I agree to interact with you." That means that if people continually disrespect your boundaries, the onus is on you to follow through. That might mean taking certain actions, or it might mean terminating your relationship with that person entirely. Either way, people will be far more likely to respect your boundaries if you yourself treat them as something to be taken seriously.

Summary:

- When we are punctual, we are showing respect for people's time. Be prepared by planning your schedule in advance, and proactive in making adjustments as soon as possible to avoid awkwardness. Create a reputation for trustworthiness by keeping your word and doing as you say you will.
- Respect other people's right to be different from you and have their own perceptions, interpretations, and opinions. Conflict is optional; rise above it. Disagree gracefully, try to hear and reflect the emotional core of what you're told, and listen for universal truths.
- Respect personal space by understanding and respecting the different proximal zones: intimate, personal, social, and public. Be aware of gender and culture differences.
- Generally, the closer the relationship, the smaller the distance, so adjust accordingly. There are strong connections between

psychological space and physical proximity. Proximity equals intimacy, so if you change the proxemic zone, you are communicating a change in degree of intimacy.
- Always, always respect a person's boundaries no matter whether or not you agree with, understand, or share their limits. Accept what you're told, don't punish or guilt people, and pay attention to nonverbal communication too.
- Communicate your own boundaries early, clearly, and assertively; don't overexplain or feel guilty; and be willing to follow through.

Part 3: Unspoken Rules of Engagement

Sometimes the greatest adventure is simply a conversation.

–Amadeus Wolfe

Chapter 9: What the "Flow" is and How to Go with It

You meet someone and you just "click." You're on the same wavelength, there's a good vibe, and the "chemistry" just works. This is *flow*—that state where conversation feels effortless.

The ironic thing about this effortlessness is that it takes some effort to achieve!

Knowing the unspoken rules of etiquette will help you go far since you'll avoid common pitfalls and prevent yourself from making the most obvious mistakes. But simply making sure you're not doing anything *wrong* is not the same as doing it *right*!

Every conversation is unique. Every time two people get together and interact, something occurs that has never occurred before. Neither of the two know what will happen; they co-create the conversation. Flow is more like a spontaneous, unfolding dance rather than a choreographed routine that is tightly controlled. And yet, those who are good conversationalists know that with a little practice and awareness, you can make these fascinating moments of connection more common.

Right now, try to think of a person with whom you've had this elusive conversational flow. Chances are you didn't have to work to get the conversation going; it just took off, and you weren't even conscious of how you chose your words or questions. Once you have a person in mind, break down the conversation's flow.

- *Who was this?*
- *Who began talking?*
- *Who said what?*
- *What was the conversation's length, setting, and backstory?*
- *When did the conversation take place (what time of day, month, year, and in what setting—for example, during a Christmas party at night).*

- *Did you know anything about the person before?*

Each of these questions will help you understand the unique context of this conversation and this person to achieve ideal conversation flow.

Next, think of the most uncomfortable conversation you've ever had. You know the kind: You couldn't get anything off the ground. There were awkward, cringe-inducing silences or weird misunderstandings. Now ask yourself the same questions you did about conversational flow. What do you notice?

Comparing your answers side by side can be revealing. Can you spot any recurring themes? Write down your immediate thoughts and see if you can identify certain factors that act as that secret conversational ingredient. Perhaps you've noticed a few things:

- Great conversations seem to happen when you least expect them, and on the spur of the moment
- They happen when people seem to be feeling *good* about themselves
- There is a certain lively back-and-forth, with no single person dominating
- It did not go the way you expected it to

- It happened when both people felt confident, safe, calm, and inspired

What does all of this tell you? Many people think that being a good conversationalist is a *performance rather than a collaboration.* **They think that in order to make others like them, they need to be witty, charming, intelligent, knowledgeable, interesting, sexy. But the truth is that none of that really matters.** If you go back and look at your most successful conversations, they had nothing to do with finding the "winner" or impressing someone with a carefully rehearsed story (in which you were the hero!).

So what does matter? Making the *other person* feel witty, charming, intelligent, and so on. The irony is that you will be perceived as a great conversationalist if you are able to truly listen and let the other person shine. A great conversation is not a lesson, a court case, a presentation, or a battle. It's a great opportunity to **connect** with another human being in the moment. That connection—and not your ego—is the most important thing. If you can make other people feel good, listened to, and important, the conversation will flow much more easily. And you'll enjoy it more too!

The Principle of Invitation and Inspiration

Sometimes, if we're lucky, the flow of a conversation seems to happen on its own. You and the other person get along well, and the conversation flows easily and feels natural. That's great when it happens . . . but what do you do when it doesn't?

Not to worry! Just because that flow and connection doesn't happen automatically, it doesn't mean it can't happen or that it's impossible to have a really enjoyable conversation with someone. This is where the **principle of invitation and inspiration** comes in. Conversations that flow easily and feel natural are naturally based on invitations and ideas.

- An **invitation** is saying something that explicitly lets your partner know it is their turn to speak.
- An **inspiration** is saying something that makes your partner want to speak without you prompting them.

Juicy conversations tend to have both of the above in abundance, but if you find yourself in a flagging conversation, you can inject one or both to get things flowing again. The big idea is to keep them talking (again, you don't save a dying conversation by talking too much *yourself*!).

With a little practice, you'll find that invitation and inspiration will help you start fun, easy conversations with just about everyone you meet. There will be far fewer awkward silences, forced transitions, or fake small talk. And that applies to the deep and meaningful conversations you have with people you're close to and the ten-second interactions with people you'll never meet again.

Let's analyze this conversation:

You: "How was your weekend?"

Your partner: "Oh, it was great. How was yours?"

You: "It was fine."

Your partner: (Cricket sounds.)

Ouch. So what happened? Well, you didn't give your partner a clear **invitation**. Your partner simply didn't know what to say next (and perhaps was unsure if it was his turn to speak.) So he didn't reply. You'll know how this feels when the shoe is on the other foot. It's like the conversation comes to a screeching halt and you're left standing there, wondering how to jumpstart it from a cold standstill. Granted, this is a pretty basic example, but variations of the above are surprisingly common, and they're absolutely flow killers.

An **invitation** is when you say something that lets your partner know it is their turn to talk, while an **inspiration** is when you say something that makes your partner want to speak up on their own. Either way, though, both are keeping things flowing because they are prompting the other person to speak. Without them, the other person won't know what to say, or else won't feel particularly moved to think of anything to say.

Take a look at this conversation:

You: "How was your weekend?"

Your partner: "Oh, it was great. How was yours?"

You: "It was amazing! I mean, other than the fact that I broke my leg."

Them: "Oh no, really? How did you do *that*?"

You: "I'm a competitive jump rope athlete, and I was attempting the Norwegian Triple Under Tuck with a front spin."

Them: "Wow. I didn't even know you could be a jump rope athletes."

You: "Neither did I until last year. Were you any good at jump rope in school?"

Them: "Actually, I was! But I don't think I've picked up a skipping rope for decades . . ."

The above conversation is *flowing*. It might not be the most thrilling topic in the world, and it's not deep and meaningful or going to change anyone's life, but it's dynamic and moving—i.e., both people feel like they *want* to contribute, and there are no awkward silences everyone is trying to fill.

"I broke my leg"—this is inspiration. Saying your weekend was amazing except for the fact that you broke a leg instantly inspires a question: How?! The other person almost can't help but asking—that sense of inevitability creates flow and ease.

"I broke my leg doing the Norwegian Triple Under Tuck . . ."—this is inspiration for the same reason. Whenever you say something unusual, unexpected, or slightly bizarre/funny, you pique the other person's interest. You signal that you are no longer grinding along the same old boring small talk pathways. This, again, creates flow.

"Were you any good at jump rope in school?"— this is an invitation. Any time you ask a question, it's an invitation. If you had continued with a third inspiration about your broken leg, it might have come across as a bit self-absorbed, but by bouncing that conversational ball back over the net, you are communicating that you are also interested in this other person, and you deliberately invite them to contribute, too. It doesn't always have to be a literal question, though. "Hm, if I were guessing, I'd say you were pretty athletic in school."

If your conversation partner is switched on, they will respond with their own invitations and inspirations, giving you plenty of time to step back into the limelight again and carry things forward. Typically, this inspiration/invitation technique is only needed to get people started in the very beginnings of conversations. Once a topic of mutual interest has been identified, the thing seems to run along on its own steam.

What if it's you who is talking to the jump rope athlete and, truth be told, you find this topic excruciatingly boring and secretly think the whole endeavor is a bit lame? Well, luckily, it doesn't matter! You can still engage with their interest in the topic and later subtly introduce your own, or listen carefully to hear for something else they might be interested in so you can steer the conversation away from jump rope:

Them: "I broke my leg doing the Norwegian Triple Under Lock."

You: "Oh my God, that's the craziest thing I've ever heard. Are you ultra-competitive about it and everything?"

Them: "Haha, no, not competitive really. But I do like to challenge myself. I think it's important to always have something you're working toward, you know?"

You: "I couldn't agree more! Last year I ran a marathon for that very reason."

Them: "Oh yeah?"

And so on. As you can see, the topic has been steered toward something you're more comfortable with (running) *without ever losing flow*. Here, the trick is that you use a question, which politely invites them to speak ("are you very competitive?") but which ultimately gives you more conversation fuel going forward.

Another option is to pay close attention and listen for topics that the other person appears to be most interested in. Clues are obvious once you pay attention: a sudden excitement in the voice, increased pace of speaking, increased pitch, more animated facial expression, closing proximal space, using more energetic hand gestures ... all of these point to a topic that is of interest and will help things flow more easily.

The Secret to Being a Good Conversationalist

It's pretty simple: **You need to care.** That's it. Not act like you care or say things that make you appear as though you care. You need to *genuinely care*.

Sounds easy, but what this amounts to is no less than a total mindset shift around how you approach conversations and other people in general. Many experts will tell you that you need to smile, make eye contact, watch your body language, and so on. But the reason they say you should do this is because these are the things you would *naturally* do if you genuinely cared.

With the right mindset, there are no bad conversations; every human being you encounter is fascinating and unique. If you really appreciate what a gift it is to encounter someone who is totally different from you and learn from them and share, then you will start to look at conversations not as difficult chores to master and manage, but as *opportunities for connection*—or even as games!

In practice, this looks like listening. Really listening. Which means turning your full and non-judgmental, non-assuming attention to the person and the world they're sharing with you. It means doing that without thinking of how you'll respond when they're done talking, or what you think about what they're sharing. It means entering into their world with curiosity, compassion, and real positive regard.

To be "good with people" does not require you to have any special skills or characteristics. But it does require a certain *orientation* to other human beings—that orientation is gentle, unselfish, and a little playful. You can make small changes toward being that person in your very next conversation. Instead of making a statement, see if you can ask a question. Pause for a few seconds longer than you ordinarily would as you take in their answer. Imagine for a few moments that you are in the presence of the most important and interesting person in the universe. You may surprise yourself to find that this quickly becomes true—giving people compassionate and undivided attention can actually be fun!

When you find your own ego rearing its head, remember to inspire and invite instead. When you feel some judgment coming on, ask a question to learn more. Try to see the universal truth behind this foreign perspective. See if you can find common ground and expand on it. If things feel a little stale or slow, prick your ears to notice little flutters of genuine emotion or interest, and then follow that by asking more questions.

There are many, many tips, tricks, and techniques out there that are designed to help you construct fruitful conversations. But none of them will mean much if you are not **connecting genuinely, emotionally, and in the present** with the unique person in front of you. So start there!

Chapter 10: Honoring the Rule of Reciprocation

In his now well-known 1984 bestseller *Influence: The Psychology of Persuasion*, Dr. Cialdini outlined what he saw as the "Six Principles of Persuasion": scarcity, authority, consistency, liking, social proof . . . and reciprocity. His theory on reciprocity has since heavily informed marketing and sale strategies, but the framework is applicable to many other forms of human interaction.

The rule of reciprocity is the idea that when someone gives you a gift, whether it's an object, a kind deed, or an act of generosity, you automatically repay it or do something nice in return. People from all cultures have a strong desire to return gifts or favors with gifts of their own. This urge comes out in things like responding to party invitations, Christmas cards, birthday gifts, or acts of kindness.

This way of doing things has existed for as long as human societies have because it helps us survive. Archaeologist Richard Leakey says that this system of giving and getting is at the heart of what makes us human. "We are human because our ancestors learned to share their food and their skills in a network of honorable obligations." And cultural anthropologists Lionel Tiger and Robin Fox say that our web of debt is a valuable tool that allows for the division of labor, the exchange of goods and services, and the creation of clusters of interdependencies that tie us together in highly efficient causal units.

There are three types of reciprocity:

- **Generalized reciprocity:** This form often involves exchanges amongst families or friends. There is no expectation of a returned favor; instead, people simply do something for another based on the belief that if the situation were reversed, the other person would do the same thing for them. This type of reciprocity is related to altruism.
- **Balanced reciprocity:** This type involves a calculation of the value of the exchange and an expectation that the favor will be returned within a specified

time frame. For example, someone might exchange something they have, whether it is a skill or tangible item, for something of perceived equal value. These calculations may be more or less conscious and communicated.

- **Negative reciprocity:** This form of reciprocity happens when one party involved in the exchange is trying to get more out of the "deal" than the other person—which obviously feels manipulative and undermines the spirit of things. Selling a much-needed item at an inflated price is one example of negative reciprocity and is likely to generate feelings of hostility and mistrust.

Marketers use a wide range of methods to get people to buy their products. Some of them are easy to understand, like sales, coupons, and special offers. Others are much sneakier and use psychological tactics that most people remain in the dark about. For example, a company might make a big deal about giving something for "free" to a prospective customer, knowing that human nature will press on that person to feel as though they now owe the company in some way . . . i.e., a future sale.

But, if we put sales and marketing tactics squarely in the "negative reciprocity" category and move on, we can use our knowledge of the other kinds to better understand unwritten social rules and learn more about etiquette in general.

In friendships, family relationships, romantic connections, and even colleague situations, good connections are built on mutuality. This is so much more than "you scratch my back and I'll scratch yours." Rather, it's about both people taking on the shared risk of assuming the other is on their side. We will look at kindness, compassion, and so on in the next section, but realize that any time you deliberately give to someone, your unspoken expectation of receiving from them in the future is there to cement the bond between you both. So, it is not about coming out on top at all or getting something for nothing. **It's really about fortifying that web of connection and representing that relationship in behavioral terms.**

The Politics of Giving and Taking

Did you know that the Old Middle Dutch root for the word "gift" is the same as that for the word "poison"? When you give someone a gift, you are in effect breaching their boundaries and intruding on their world—albeit in a good way. But just as cultures all over the world understand that a gift can also be an insult, a curse, or a threat, we need to be aware that **any act of giving has the potential to change the dynamics of a relationship and is as clear an act of communication as eye contact or physical touch.**

There is a universal human tendency to be fair, to reciprocate, and to engage in mutually beneficial interactions. But doing so often puts us in vulnerable positions, which means that relationships of all kinds demand risk. When we take that risk away, we signal a willingness to connect that builds trust with others over time. Some would say that this is all a relationship really is—an ongoing agreement to trust and depend on one another.

Sadly, if people were always kind and altruistic, there would be no need for certain etiquette rules. But in the real world, it pays to be aware of when giving and taking can veer into exploitative, obligatory, or manipulative giving. When the rules of reciprocity are violated, unlimited drama that can result.

A literal gift is the most obvious manifestation of give and take, and there are plenty of rules around good conduct when it comes to gifts. But reciprocity takes on many more subtle forms that it's worth being cognizant of. Most of the time, conscious giving and taking comes down to clear expectations, open communication, and—you guessed it—respect.

Every relationship has the potential for reciprocity. Let's take a closer look.

Close Relationships—Family and Partners

Families have different rules about how to treat each other. Some families want to be paid back right away, while others don't keep track of who did what when. It's important to know how family members feel about reciprocity, because when expectations aren't clear, relationships can end. In other words, even though it would be easier, try not to make any assumptions. For example, imagine a sibling gives another sibling a big sum of money to buy something. Months later, they feel it's taking too long for them to be paid back. Meanwhile, the other sibling had no idea that they were even expected to pay it back, let alone when. A fight ensues.

In many ways, family relationships can be more conflictual precisely because people are too quick to make assumptions. Many families bumble along for decades with one person thinking, "Oh, he never expects anything at

Christmas; he hates all that fuss," and the other seething in resentment, thinking, "He's always been rude like that, snubbing me every single Christmas." It may feel a tiny bit awkward, but it's usually better to talk openly and directly about expectations for things like:

- Wishes, cards, and gifts for birthdays, celebrations, and anniversaries
- Taking turns when hosting or feeding people
- The rules about "favors"

The default unspoken rule is that you return a kindness. If you can, return it "in kind," i.e., do something that will be perceived of roughly equal value and of the same type. DO NOT return a kindness with something much larger than what was originally given, or else you risk creating awkwardness, feelings of obligation, or never-ending gift chains that people feel unable to break! Likewise, keep the kindness of the same type. If your mother baked you a beautiful cake, give her a nice bottle of wine—not a new deluxe toaster.

What about spouses and romantic partners? The single biggest mistake you can make here is to assume that the rule of reciprocity doesn't apply. It does! In close, trusting partnerships, people often wait months or even years to get "paid back" and may be more than willing to give huge leeway in the kind of repayment they receive. But if you consistently ignore the need for balance and fairness, expect that over time, resentment will build or the person will slowly begin to believe that you don't care.

An important point here: the *form* that a kindness takes can vary enormously in close and trusting relationships. For example, one partner might give emotional support, while the other gives financial stability. One person will splash out on an expensive gift, and the other will dedicate their time or make something by hand that is unique and deeply sentimental. The closer the relationship, the more room there is for these sorts of "negotiations." What matters most is that both people feel that sufficient efforts are being made and that the other person is paying attention and that the spirit of giving is there. This is often why a wealthy person giving an expensive gift they can easily afford is usually *not* seen as a very valuable contribution in a romantic relationship.

Friends

Again, it's important for friends to talk about what they expect from each other because everyone has different ideas about how long it should take to pay back. For instance, some people think that when you go out with friends for dinner or drinks, they will naturally take turns paying. In other groups of friends, it is expected that if one person pays the bill, everyone else should chip in with their share right away.

When there is no exchange of money, such as when time and emotional support are being given, the giver might not expect to be paid back until they are in the same situation. For others, they may not expect any kindness to be returned at all—but they do expect to be thanked profusely and for you to clearly and fully acknowledge the effect their help has had on you.

It's not a question of what is "right" or not, but rather that everyone is on the same page so that misunderstandings don't have a chance to crop up.

With friends of all kinds, it's generally safe to assume that if you give, you have a right to expect to receive, although not necessarily immediately. If you are invited to someone's house, take it as a given that the next meeting of that kind should take place at your house. If a friend lends you a power tool, thank them and make it clear that they can borrow your things, too, when the time comes. There's no need to fall over yourself to immediately return a kindness—in fact, doing so can come across badly. But do acknowledge the "debt" and remember it, paying back when it's your turn without fanfare or argument.

Coworkers

Relationships at work tend to be more formal, so follow the *immediate exchange rule*—unless your coworkers are also friends (beware, though: the coworker/friend line can be a blurry one, so be crystal clear that your colleagues are indeed friends and not just super polite colleagues). Here, the goal is to pay back as soon as possible and be perfectly fair. Making people wait strains trust and patience and may make demands of people that extend beyond their goodwill toward you. For colleagues, it's almost always better to split restaurant bills there and then and clear any unspoken "debts" quickly. If someone lends you money because you left your wallet at home, pay them back that very afternoon when you get home.

One final potential pitfall: do not be overgenerous. Over-givers can sometimes try to alleviate anxiety by doing too much, but this can in fact put people in awkward positions. If there is a "Secret Santa" at work, for example, and the budget is ten dollars, don't buy a thirty-dollar gift. It is just as much a violation of reciprocity to over-give than to under-give! In the same vein, do not give large or personal gifts to work colleagues or bosses unless there is some special reason to. It makes sense to contribute as a work team to a colleague's birthday; however, privately sending an expensive gift unbidden can be perceived as boundary-breaking and can create an awkward need for the recipient to reciprocate.

In closing, here are a few final give-and-take unspoken social rules that will help you navigate gift-giving situations:

- If given a gift, open it there and then unless told not to. Smile, say thank you, and express gratitude *even if you really hate it*!
- For larger gifts, especially those given for big occasions, it's polite to send a thank-you card.
- Never sell a gift or regift it to someone else.
- Never ask for a gift to be returned, or behave as though it's still yours.
- Never give a gift or do a favor for someone with the expressed intention of getting something out of them in return. Be honest if you are giving a gift or doing

a good turn *only* because you are trying to assuage guilty feelings, feel obliged, or hope that it will increase emotional closeness. Even though the rule of reciprocation applies, try to give without expectation of return.
- Do not break a person's boundaries in order to help them. If they are ill and want to be left alone, honor that boundary and don't force yourself on them under the guise of being kind and giving.

Chapter 11: Gratitude, Manners, and Kindness

Few people make the connection between compassion, gratitude, and manners. We tend to think of kindness as something saintly, generous, and warm, whereas we may see manners as something polite, stiff, and ultimately fake. But really, they are the same concept—only expressed in different ways.

Compassion, gratitude, and good manners all have significant overlap.

If we have genuine empathy and consideration for our fellow human beings, we are able to think about them and their needs; we engage with them in reciprocal give and take, and when we say "thank you" to them, we pause to really experience that moment of gratitude. Think of manners as a kind of social scaffolding onto which you can build real feelings of both gratitude and generosity (hint: they come from the same place!).

Grateful people are more likely to feel appreciative in a wider range of situations and recognize the good deeds of others. When you are thankful for something and truly receive it as a gift, you are giving the gift of that gratitude and happiness to the people who have helped you feel that way—and everyone loves to feel needed like this!

Psychologists Dr. Robert A. Emmons of the University of California, Davis, and Dr. Michael E. McCullough of the University of Miami were the first to compile fascinating research on the power of gratitude (2003), but more and more research is proving that being thankful has positive effects on just about every area of life. This creates a positive, self-reinforcing feedback loop: **The more gratitude we show, the better we feel and the less likely we are to take things for granted or complain and the more likely we are to be grateful. Plus, the more grateful we are, the more inclined others are to help us since they can tell that their efforts really do make a difference.**

How we show gratitude depends a lot on the social situation. For example, taking a partner to their favorite restaurant to thank them for their support might be a good way to show gratitude, but it obviously wouldn't be a good way to show gratitude to a stranger who held a door open for us. The feeling of happiness and gratitude is the same, and it's genuine—but etiquette and manners are the rules that dictate *how we express that feeling appropriately.*

Gratitude Causes Generosity Causes Gratitude

Polite, courteous people tend to have an aura of positivity about them. When you stop to really notice just how much you have to be thankful for, it seems to grow in your awareness. By simply acknowledging these things and saying "thank you" out loud, you seem to increase them. And the more you believe you have, the more likely you are to want to share it with others. This is how gratitude can foster feelings of generosity . . . which in turn creates give-and-take dynamics with others in which there is yet more to be thankful for.

Start with gratitude. This goes far beyond just saying thank you! Turn your awareness outside of yourself and notice all the little things that occur in your life that don't necessarily have to be there but are. The clear blue sky. A delicious cup of hot coffee. The parcel you ordered arriving at your house on time. Your colleague taking a message for you while you were out. Your partner remembering to pick up your favorite snack at the store. A bird singing outside the window.

These days, the "gratitude journal" idea is well known, but you don't need to literally sit down with pen and paper to start reaping the benefits of a more grateful mindset. All it takes is for you to regularly pause, become aware, and notice all the things that are actually going pretty well for you. It may even be possible that you start noticing the good in situations you were previously unhappy about. You've had an argument with your parents, but at least the air is clear now and everyone is on the same page. You had a car accident and it was awful, but there's little damage. That guy at work is super annoying, but if you're being kind, you can see he means well. And so on.

What does this have to do with unspoken social rules?

Well, when you are continuously cultivating a grateful and positive attitude, you instantly communicate that to everyone you encounter, even if only on an unconscious level. You convey a mindset of hopeful cooperation, self-regulation, and happiness—

and that's always going to make any interaction more positive.

But it goes deeper than this. A person who is grateful is a person who is *not* fearful, grasping, selfishb or greedy. Think about it: If you have what you need (even more than what you need), it is so much easier to share, to give, and to cooperate. You are not coming from a place of lack or insecurity. You can show up to every conversation with calm curiosity and generosity, rather than a fearful self-focus or a thinly veiled attempt to see what you can get out of it.

Show our gratitude by regularly saying thank you. Thank people even if you will never see them again. Make eye contact, be sincere, and let them know the impact they've had. Can you recall ever being thanked sincerely in this way? It felt good, right? Give that same gift to someone else.

Say thank you even if the person was only doing their job. Tip generously and give compliments. Let other people know how their efforts have made your life easier. In a professional context, leave good reviews or pass on contact details when making a recommendation. Introduce two people in your network who you think need to know one another. Use "thank you" to start a conversation—people feel seen and validated when you sincerely inquire about them, their work, their process, and what certain actions mean to them. Your interest is a genuine way of showing your thankfulness.

Give bonuses to employees if they've been loyal. If it's appropriate, visit people to say thank you or give a gift. You might find it easier to write a note or even a full-blown letter. Your simple act of recognition could spur an entire friendship or be the start of a fruitful business relationship. You may find that people are compelled to work even harder to help you in the future.

So here we see an interesting paradox: If you are able to be truly grateful for what you have and focus on fostering that feeling in yourself, you indirectly bring that feeling of generosity to others. In this way, gratitude and kindness are almost contagious. When you treat yourself well, you make it more likely that you treat others the same way, and those good feelings spread. Congratulations—you are creating for yourself the kind of world that you'd most like to live in.

Random Acts of Kindness

One of the best ways to express gratitude is to share your good fortune and be generous to others, i.e., a random act of kindness.

Guess what . . . good manners *are* random acts of kindness!

Saying please and thank you, holding the door, smiling and making friendly eye contact, or helping a stranger pick up something they've dropped are all some of the sincerest ways to spread compassion in the world. One of the best things you can do to lift your own mood is to be kind to someone you don't know, for no reason at all, even if it would be just as easy to ignore them. As John F. Kennedy reminded us, "We express our gratitude, we must never forget that the highest appreciation is not to utter words, but to live by them."

Try some of the following and see how powerful a shift in mindset it brings:

- In a coffee shop, pay for the person behind you or leave a tip for the baristas.

- Challenge yourself to smile at three random people who catch your eye while out in public today.
- Go through clutter at home and make up a bag of items to donate to charity.
- The next time you're at the laundromat or using a vending machine or paying for parking, leave a few coins behind as a nice surprise for whoever comes after you.
- Scroll through your contacts list and look to see who you haven't reached out to in a while. Pick three people and send them a sweet message.
- At work, think of something someone has done for you and thank them and praise them for their efforts.
- Leave a positive online review or get in touch with a business to let them know that a particular employee really impressed you. There's no telling how influential your feedback could be.
- Volunteer. It doesn't necessarily have to be at an animal shelter or soup kitchen, either. See if your local school needs help with anything or ask around at a church or community center. Sometimes, all it takes is volunteering some of your time and expertise doing rather ordinary tasks—it still makes a big difference, though.

- Think of someone you're angry with or still holding a grudge against. Ask if you can gracefully let go of it and move on. You don't even have to share this with them if you're not ready. But forgiveness is a powerful gift, for us *and* for them.
- Look around your world and ask yourself how everyone is doing. Is there someone who is quietly struggling and could use extra support? Is there something you have or know that could make someone else's life easier. Don't wait for them to ask—just step in and help.
- If you encounter a funny video or meme or an interesting article, send a link to someone.
- Instead of just Googling things like recipes or DIY tricks, ask the older people in your life for help and advice. They'll feel honored that you esteem their opinion, and you may very well learn something.
- When you've done something wrong, apologize immediately and completely. This might not seem like an act of kindness, but if done with sincerity at the right moment, it can ironically be one of the best ways to deepen trust and respect in any relationship (we'll look at apologies more in a later chapter).

- Do something nice for someone without them knowing. Donate anonymously, leave a secret gift somewhere for someone to find, or privately sing someone's praises to a third person. You're spreading a bit of goodness in the world.

Try to use manners and etiquette as a kind of social prompt to be more conscious of other people's needs and inject a little more compassion into everyday life. When you thank a waitress or cashier, don't just mouth the words without thinking—literally try to make that brief human connection and see if you can really feel and convey that sense of gratitude. Add in a smile and some eye contact or even have a quick and friendly conversation if it seems appropriate.

When you receive a gift or a favor from someone, mentally make a note right there to do something nice for them later on (or you can literally make a note if you're likely to forget!). Keep a small book or calendar with people's birthdays and anniversaries in it, or set reminders on your phone to regularly reach out to others and check in on them. Pay attention so that whenever you next meet someone, you know exactly what to enquire about: "I've been meaning to ask, how is your mother after her operation?" or "So how did the big camping trip pan out?"

Do your best to pay attention when you're told small family details or the names and ages of people's children. Most people tune out when boring information like this is shared, but grab hold of it, reflect it, and you may find it's not boring at all but a way to enter into more interesting conversation with time. This simple act of remembering what you're told and showing an interest in it is a profound act of kindness in a world where most of us are completely self-absorbed in our own problems. Try to imagine that everyone you encounter is wearing a sign on their head that says "make me feel important." Sounds cheesy, but just a few shifts in this direction will translate into compassion and kindness that people can really feel. You'll come across as likeable, trustworthy, and kind—and people will want to keep being around you.

Finally, one way to think about becoming more compassionate is to imagine that it's the same as becoming more *aware*. Many people think that being kind is a question of generosity. They think that giving to charities or volunteering is a compassionate thing to do—and it is. However, real kindness is a living, breathing

thing. And most of all, it is **responsive** to other people's emerging needs in the moment.

Consider situation A: you know your friend is struggling with money at the moment, and when you're out with them one day at a café, you notice them pick up a muffin but sadly put it down again as they claim they're "not hungry after all." Knowing your friend well and paying close attention to their body language and facial expression, you realize that this is a cover and that, in reality, they're trying to save money. But you also know you would humiliate your friend to say you noticed this, and it would make them uncomfortable to know you felt compelled to be charitable to them. So, you decide to quietly buy the same muffin, claiming it's for you, then later say it's too big to finish and beg your friend to *help you* by finishing it.

Let's unpack the situation: You paid attention to your friend, noticing their behavior, "listening" to and being alert to their needs. You also had the presence of mind to realize the potential awkwardness of offering to pay, thus bringing attention to the thing they're embarrassed about. You step in and find a way to make your friend's life a little easier and more enjoyable, but without making a big performance out of it. This also means your friend is not forced to make a big show of their gratitude.

Compare it to situation B: You want to do something good for the community, so you donate a big box of muffins to the local soup kitchen, who serve them later that day.

Both of these are compassionate, kind acts of generosity. But situation A shows a *responsiveness* and care that situation B doesn't. That's because it comes from a place of attention and recognition and speaks directly a need that is emerging in the real world. Big difference! You already know that it's a good thing to listen to people in conversation. Well, listening is also the start of genuine compassion. Today, see if you can listen out for people's needs, and see what you can do for them. Does anyone need help? Information? Support? Attention? Small gestures offered at exactly the right moment can feel more valuable than winning the lottery!

Chapter 12: Humor Etiquette

Imagine a person who is sociable, charming, and good in conversations. Are you imagining someone quite entertaining and funny?

A good sense of humor is like magic fairy dust. It relaxes you, removes the stress from a situation, and has the potential to turn tense moments around to your benefit. That wonderful sense of flow and connection are turbo-charged when people are laughing and having a good time. A person who can laugh at themselves and get others to laugh will be perceived as confident, likeable, fun, and even attractive. A sense of humor is a kind of social display that communicates an ease with life and a certain resilience and good health. It is positively *magnetic*.

However, because humor is such potent stuff, it's easy to get things wrong. Very wrong. If you've ever had a big argument that began with the words "but it was only a joke!" then you know how badly wrong that can be.

The only way to truly understand humor is from the perspective of the person being joked about. Yes, making jokes and being funny is something you do to put yourself at ease and make yourself look good, but the moment you make others feel uncomfortable, you've failed, and it doesn't matter how funny you think something is or how unreasonable you think the other person is for not agreeing with you.

Don't be that person who stubbornly insists that they just have a "dark sense of humor" or that other people are merely too sensitive or don't get you. A pretty obvious unspoken rule is that if other people aren't laughing, you're not being funny—you're just being rude.

According to Steve Wilson, who is a self-titled "joyologist," comedian, and psychologist, there are seven golden rules for wielding a charming sense of humor without the risk of alienating or upsetting people. He considers humor the "shock absorber of life"!

Rule 1: When in doubt, leave it out. Just like with compassion, be aware of who you're talking to. Know who they are, what they like, and what amuses/impresses them. Also be aware of the dynamic between you both, your relative positions, and the degree of formality of the situation. Context is everything.

Using humor that's at odds with your position will hit awkwardly. Jokes that land well with your friends may flop with family or customers; "inside" jokes are seldom amusing for those who were not party to their creation. The rule of thumb is this: if you're not sure whether what you're about to say is inappropriate, err on the side of saying nothing.

Rule 2: Timing is key. What's tragic one moment can be pretty funny two weeks later. But when joking about potentially sensitive matters, it's best to wait rather than make fun of something when it's "too soon." Humor can lighten dark moods, but you have to be really careful. If you can see the humor in a bad situation but you're unsure, you could gently suggest, "I can totally see us laughing our heads off about this in about two weeks' time . . ." Better yet, first wait for an indication from the other person that they're ready to start laughing about a difficult topic.

Rule 3: Don't make fun of people. Chances are, you're not a professional comedian. And even *they* get into hot water for going too far! Insults and teasing are lazy humor. Even if the other person is laughing in the moment, you can never be sure that you haven't actually offended them. Even if you haven't, their opinion of you may drop imperceptibly, and you may have lost their trust and respect without even realizing it.

According to Wilson, there is such a thing as "humor abuse." He claims that racial or sexist jokes, put-downs, embarrassment, sarcasm, and ridicule can all do serious damage—especially to children.

Rule 4: Don't try to be edgy. Some people can't imagine what humor looks like if it doesn't contain taboo language or skirt around contentious topics. But really, these people lack imagination! The truth is, you can never predict how people will respond to swearing, "toilet humor," or risqué language. You might get a laugh, or you might seriously damage that connection. It's not worth the risk.

At least until you're really, really certain about your audience's tolerance levels, leave out the edgy stuff, don't joke about the sex-politics-religion triad, and steer clear of emotive topics that could quickly swing into bad territory. Good humor doesn't have to have a nasty edge to it. You don't need to be a clever wise-cracking social commentator. Try instead to just put people at ease and communicate acceptance, warmth, and comfort. If you can make fun of *situations and not people*, your humor will draw everyone together, deepen connection, and be genuinely fun for everyone. Push the limits and you may only create more division and guardedness—which is the last thing you want.

What about Sarcasm?

Great. Sarcasm. Just brilliant. Nobody's ever tried *that* before.

Sarcasm is difficult to define, but we all know it when we see it. The official definition is: the use of irony to mock or convey contempt. The "irony" part is simply that we are saying the opposite of what we mean. The effect is a jarring discrepancy—that discrepancy can be pretty funny, or it can be felt as a sharp sting delivered with the intention to insult. So how can you use sarcasm to be funny rather than hurtful?

The answer is: very carefully.

You've probably heard it said that "sarcasm is the lowest form of wit." Is this true? Well, that depends on how you do it. Here are two

main differences between good sarcasm and bad sarcasm.

Rule 1: Bad sarcasm is about avoidance; good sarcasm is about engagement

The British sense of humor is rife with the kind of sarcasm that escalates amusement in a situation rather than kills it. Watch classic British comedies and sitcoms and see how sarcasm is used to *exaggerate* situations and make them funnier ("Oh, you've made dinner! Excellent. I love a challenge.") JK Rowling writes the following conversation in *Harry Potter, Order of the Phoenix,*

"'What were you doing under our window, boy?'
'Listening to the news,' said Harry in a resigned voice.
His aunt and uncle exchanged looks of outrage.
'Listening to the news! Again?'
'Well, it changes every day, you see,' said Harry."

Bad sarcasm, however, doesn't lean into a situation but evades it. It can be difficult to pinpoint subtle things like tone and intention, but sarcasm has failed if it doesn't add levity and a fun bit of absurdity, but rather feels like a steel door being shut in someone's face.

"Hey, do you need some help?"
"Help? Help? Oh, no, really, I just *love* having to carry all this by myself" (plus eyeroll).

Rule 2: Good sarcasm mocks the self or the situation; bad sarcasm hurts others

On a walk in the woods, you encounter a dilapidated wood shack, and you say to your friend, "Man, if I get a raise one day, I could just about afford a place like *that*." Your friend will likely laugh because you're the butt of your own joke. If you said, "Hey, look, a spacious one-room studio apartment with a gorgeous landscaped garden and great ventilation . . . fifteen hundred dollars a month, excluding utilities," then you wouldn't be mocking a person at all, but rather a general situation. It would also be pretty funny. If you think about it beforehand, you can turn almost any insult or jab into a good-natured joke about an idea or concept rather than a specific person's failings.

Okay, so what do you do if you have accidentally put your foot in your mouth and said something that hurt someone's feelings? Well, that's easy: apologize. Try not to explain, justify, or excuse, and avoid arguing with the other person about whether they're justified in their offense or not. You'll get nowhere trying to convince them that their hurt feelings are actually imaginary, anyway. Is it possible that some people *are* too sensitive and perhaps even claim offense as a way to manipulate and dominate a situation? Sure. But again, you gain nothing by suggesting this and will only embroil yourself further in awkwardness and unpleasantness.

You: "Man, if I get a raise one day, I could just about afford a place like *that*."
Them: "Actually, homelessness is a real problem in this city, and many people are forced every day to sleep in places like that. You are really privileged to earn the salary you do . . ."
You: "Oh. You know what, you're right. Sorry, I didn't mean any offense" (quickly changes the topic and makes a mental note that this topic is a sensitive one for that person).

As long as you keep in mind that humor is there as a social lubricant and as a tool to create connection, then it's easy to just drop it if it's in fact having the opposite effect. Today, the social and political landscape can feel positively boobytrapped with potential offense and conversational landmines that would have been considered harmless only a few years ago. But ultimately, it doesn't matter. A good conversationalist can navigate *any* social situation with awareness, tact, kindness, and good humor and maintain that human connection—even in an atmosphere fraught with social division!

Using Humor to Deflect Awkwardness

Used poorly, humor can hurt people and make situations painfully awkward and uncomfortable. Used wisely, humor can be a secret weapon for eliminating awkwardness.

Consider this brief exchange:

A: "You're almost thirty. When are you going to get married, huh?"
B: "Oh, damn! I knew there was something I forgot to put on my to-do list!"

It's funny. The reason it's funny is because it provides some welcome relief and discharge of tension created by A in asking such a rude question. Here's the great thing about humor—it can defuse conflict and cause a bad conversation to do an immediate one eighty. Being a witty person is about so much more than just avoiding saying an offensive thing. It's about using humor to its fullest potential—i.e., as a way to smooth ruffled feathers, crumble resistance, and wriggle out of potentially unpleasant snags in conversation.

Sometimes, humor is in fact the best way to deal with a bully, artfully disarming their escalation and quickly steering the conversation somewhere healthier. If you're dealing with someone unpleasant, a well-timed moment of humor can be a very clever way of getting them to back off—without stooping to their level or breaking etiquette.

The legendary "witty comeback" is the stuff of good comedy, but it's something you can practice, too, if you are mindful enough to *not rise to a provocation*. In the above exchange, Person B could easily have shown their hurt and annoyance by "taking the bait" and getting engaged in a heavy conversation about minding their own business. Instead, they breeze past it and use the opportunity to their own advantage, likely providing those listening something amusing to listen to and getting Person A to quickly back down.

One unexpectedly powerful way to do this is via self-deprecation. The idea is that if you yourself are comfortable putting yourself in a position of perceived weakness, it takes all the fun out of it for the other person to keep trying to! Consider this example:

"Look at this room! It's a pigsty!"

"Don't be ridiculous, a pig couldn't stand to live in my room."

Here, humor completely stops short a potential argument or judgment. The second person not only doesn't fight back, they take the insult and run with it to the extreme, making it funny. The result is that the potential bad feelings evaporate. Even if the second person did acknowledge the criticism and decided to give their room a clean after all, they did so with much less friction and awkwardness than if they had responded seriously.

Summary:

- Conversational flow is that state of enjoyment and ease that requires your focus on the other person rather than your own ego.
- Use the principle of inspiration as an invitation to jump start conversational flow. An invitation is saying something that explicitly lets your partner know it is their turn to speak. An inspiration is saying something that makes your partner want to speak without you prompting them.
- The secret to good conversation is to genuinely care and to listen to what you're told. Be receptive and non-judgmental, ask questions, and show interest.

- The rule of reciprocity is the idea that when someone gives you a gift, whether it's an object, a kind deed, or an act of generosity, you automatically repay it or do something nice in return. Generosity is about fortifying the webs of social connection. Always return a favor; family or personal relationships often have more relaxed expectations on that return, but it is still required.
- Gratitude, manners, and kindness all have significant overlap. The more gratitude we show, the better we feel and the less likely we are to take things for granted or complain, and the more likely we are to be grateful. We also increase feelings of generosity since we are not coming from a place of fear or insecurity. Instead, try random acts of kindness and be aware of and responsive to people's needs.
- Humor is a powerful way to deflect tension. But never use humor to harm others; steer clear of sarcasm, mockery, and contentious topics when making jokes.

Part 4: When Things Don't Go to Plan

Humility is not thinking less of yourself, it's thinking of yourself less.

–CS Lewis

Chapter 13: Navigating Social Misfires

Here's a riddle: What does everyone love to give but nobody wants to receive?

Unsolicited advice!

Do you sometimes give advice that wasn't asked for? If most of us were being honest, we'd say yes. It's not like we're sitting there lecturing people and telling them how to run their lives, but we nevertheless make "suggestions" and observations about what someone else should do, without thinking whether it's what the other person actually wants or needs.

Avoid Unsolicited Advice

The unspoken rule for advice and suggestions is this: **It's not your intention that counts, but how you are perceived.** In other words, no matter how well-meaning we think we are being, giving advice that isn't wanted can feel annoying, rude, and even manipulative by other people.

Unsolicited advice can be very obvious and direct, but also pretty subtle. It can come across as pretty harmless, but it can also seem passive aggressive or make you seem condescending. The irony is that in our assuming we know best about a person's situation, we immediately shut down and stop truly listening—our empathy flies out the window.

There is an asymmetry here. Most of us don't want people to talk **at** us and expound on what we should do, yet most of us find it tempting to do this very thing to others. It is impolite and arrogant to insert one's ideas and opinions into someone else's world. It conveys an unearned air of superiority because it presumes the advice-giver knows what is correct, and the advice-receiver is somehow ignorant, mistaken, or helpless. Yup, it can be really annoying!

Good etiquette and manners require us to be mindful of our primary role in conversation: to connect and create rapport. It is NOT to educate someone, help them, guide them, or preach so they see the light and come round to what we already know to be true. Approach conversations with this attitude and you will bore and alienate people—even if you don't outright say, "Here's my advice..."

By the way, **someone telling you their problems is not the same as them asking for your advice.** It is very seldom a request for a solution or a lecture. Almost always, people share their challenges because they want to be heard and understood, to be validated, and to have someone support their difficulty. It's *this* that allows them to process their problems themselves—not advice.

Too many good relationships are derailed by a subtle but disruptive power dynamic that expresses itself in unsolicited advice. Often, people create distance, misunderstandings, or awkwardness when one or both overstep and take on this advice-giving role. To avoid this, consider a few more unspoken rules when engaging with other people's problems:

Show unconditional positive regard, non-judgment, compassion, and empathy.

This is your first duty. Simply listen and validate their experience by asking questions to help you understand. Many people unconsciously treat a show of vulnerability in others with a strange glee because *they* would never be so foolish as to get into difficulties. Of course, the other person will sense this smugness, even if it's subtle. It's the quickest way to kill trust and authenticity. The best way to make sure that you don't communicate a feeling of being better than them is to *genuinely not feel that way*! And yes, that includes making a big show of being a wise and vulnerable guru on a throne, being consulted for their sagely counsel . . .

Don't tell them what they should or shouldn't do, or what they should or shouldn't think.

We all do this more often than we realize, and it can be incredibly invalidating.

"Don't say that about yourself! You're awesome!"
"You have nothing to be worried about."
"Whatever you do, don't call him back."
"You'd have to be crazy to go for that."

"You're overthinking it."
"Sleep on it, and in the morning, you'll feel differently."

Most of the time, we mean well. But when we start to dictate, judge, and assume, we *stop* listening and empathizing. Instead, ask questions and affirm what you're told.

"I feel like such a failure."
"I understand."

One alternative is just to share your own experiences but framed as our experiences—not as lessons for them to learn from.

"I remember when I was declared bankrupt last year. It nearly broke me. But I realized that the experience itself was nothing compared to how much I was beating myself up!"

Studies among college students conducted by Reeshad Dalal and Silvia Bonaccio found that "informational-based advice" was preferred and considered the most helpful. People like advice that gives them information because it makes them feel like they are autonomous and capable of making their own choices.

"My financial advisor saved my bacon back then. I'll put you in touch with her if you'd like.

If you don't work with her, she still might have some useful information on what steps to take next."

Ask if they want to hear it!

"I have some ideas about what might be helpful. Would you be interested in hearing them?"

How much unsolicited advice would be avoided by simply asking first! Try:

"Are you open to a suggestion?"

"I've been through something similar. Can I tell you about what worked for me?"

"Is there anything you'd like me to do to help?"

Finally, don't take it personally.

They asked for your advice, you gave it, and then . . . they did the opposite. Don't be offended. They owe you nothing, and if you're honest, there's nothing to say that your advice was the objective best thing to do. Don't let it bother you, and don't assume they have bad judgment or that they don't value your opinion just because they chose to do something else. In fact, be glad that they thought for themselves!

Knowing When to Back Off

Let's consider something that is a little uncomfortable to acknowledge at times. Let's say that you have worked hard on your people skills and have become the picture of good manners, etiquette, and social grace. Let's say that you're funny, empathetic, interesting to talk to, and a good listener. You're respectful and a pro at navigating all the complex and invisible rules of interaction that stump others. Let's also imagine that you encounter someone new whom you're interested in getting to know better . . . and they aren't interested.

Ouch. Here's one unspoken rule that can be difficult to swallow: **No matter what, we are never entitled to people's approval, liking, time, or attention.** Yup—even if we do everything "right."

For those of us who are a little more socially awkward, it can be excruciating to deal with the fact that some people, well, just don't like us. It might be that they're just not interested in chatting right now, or it may be that they don't want to talk *ever*. Either way, when someone doesn't want to interact with us, that is well and truly that—we cannot make them. And that's okay.

But the cruel irony is that unless someone is really blunt, politeness means that people will seldom say outright, "I don't want to talk to you." This means that we have to do some of the work and figure it out ourselves. We need to read between the lines and understand when our company is not wanted or appropriate. Have you ever known someone *you* didn't like, but they never seemed to take the hint? Well, read on to see how you can avoid making that same mistake yourself.

Watch body language. Increasing proximal distance, leaning back, and turning the body away are all strong hints. Watch also for "closed" body language like crossed arms (that is, unless it's freezing outside!). Yawning, fidgeting, staring with glazed-over eyes, sitting stiff or immobile, and staring at the floor are all bad signs, too. Sometimes, a person will linger in a conversation because they feel like they have to, but there will be small "tells," such as clenched fists or constantly flickering the eyes away from the conversation.

Be mindful online. Try not to read too much into the fact that people don't reply instantly or leave you on read. The "rules" here are so variable as to be meaningless, so don't assume anything. For some people, taking two days to reply to a WhatsApp message is normal and means nothing, whereas for others, it's basically a declaration of war. For some, a phone call is polite and preferable; for others, it's torture. How do you deal with all these different expectations? Communicate clearly yourself, don't take things personally or start reading into every detail, and try to establish proper face-to-face communication as often/soon as possible. Don't be afraid to actively ask what people's preferences are.

Pay attention to emerging patterns. Are you constantly the one initiating conversation? Are you the one who is talking the most? Are they always the one to end conversations? Do you always feel like you are leading somehow or unconsciously trying to entertain them? Do they constantly let things fall flat with one-word answers? Do they ignore questions and leave statements uncommented on? Are they actively disagreeing and arguing with everything you say? Are they avoiding eye contact?

All of these paint a picture of someone who is simply not as invested in the conversation as you are. Now, this doesn't mean that they are dying inside and want to escape as soon as possible, or that they dislike you, only that they're not interested, and it's probably not worth continuing to pursue dialogue.

Not sure? There's one way to test if a person really is keen on continuing the conversation, and it's simple. **Just stop for a moment and see if they do anything at all to keep things going.** Create a small silence and see if they make efforts to fill it, or step back a small amount to see if they subtly move to close that distance again. If so, then they are interested in talking, but they may be sending mixed signals because they're tired, distracted, shy, or just bad at expressing themselves! If not, then you can gracefully end the conversation and move on.

Dealing with Rejection

One of the most common but unpleasant "social misfires" you'll encounter is simply not getting on with someone. The uncomfortable reality we must all face is that even if we follow all the etiquette rules, even if we're nice and polite and interesting and respectful, it doesn't mean that other people will like us or want to be with us. After all, ask yourself if *you* want to be close friends with every person you meet, and you'll see very quickly that it's not feasible.

So, even if you are a practiced social butterfly, at some point or other, you're going to extend yourself to someone ... and the effort will not be reciprocated. Here, "rejection" sounds pretty dramatic, but it can simply be a mismatch of intentions in a social situation, whether professional or personal. You invite someone out, and they say they're busy. You flirt with someone, and they let you know they're not interested. You ask for feedback and support from a would-be mentor at work, and they're a little cold with you ...

The unspoken rule here is simple but hard to remember: **Don't take it personally!**

If you're disappointed or feeling a little rebuffed, pull back and give yourself a moment to feel that. It's only human to start wondering if you've done something wrong, but see if you can deliberately remind yourself that there are two sides to every interaction—and you are not responsible for other people, their boundaries, their wants, their preferences ... even their rudeness, if that's the case! You are only responsible for yourself. So take a moment to check in with yourself—have you communicated clearly, been kind, respectful, reasonable? If so, then forget it and move on.

For example, your sister-in-law seems like an interesting person, and you keep trying to befriend her, inviting her out, sending her messages, and gravitating toward her at family functions so you can chat. She continues to be cold and disinterested. Instead of wondering what it all means and feeling hurt that she doesn't like you, pull back gracefully and accept that she isn't interested and that *this means nothing about you as a person.*

Likewise, if you're dating and you meet someone you really click with, only for them to tell you a few dates in that they don't feel any chemistry, accept that gracefully and detach. It's not about you! Remind yourself that everyone has been rejected before, and you will survive! Be polite, communicate clearly, and move on.

Chapter 14: The Art of Saying NO . . . Nicely

At some point, you will be the one to issue that rejection. Bearing in mind how horrible it can be on the receiving end of rejection (even tiny rejection!), be especially mindful here of conducting yourself with respect and kindness and communicating as clearly as possible.

Declining an Invitation

Have you ever been invited somewhere but were unable to accept? Well, an invitation is just that—an invitation, not a summons! That means you are always, always entitled to turn it down if you wish. That is, **as long as you do so in a way that is sincere, follows proper protocol, and shows respect for the person who extended the invitation to you**.

As with so many unspoken etiquette rules, the right behavior becomes clear when you put yourself in the other person's shoes. They invited you for a reason: They want you to be there! This can be easy to forget. We may assume that the invitation doesn't mean much or that we were invited out of politeness. We might imagine that we won't be missed. But think about any party you've hosted—even if it was an enormous guest list, you probably felt disappointed when someone couldn't come. If they simply ignored the invitation entirely and never pitched up, you were probably quite hurt, right?

The most important thing is to **respond to any invitation as quickly and courteously as possible.** Letting people know the day before whether you can come or not signals a strong disrespect for their time. Extending an invitation to someone is an act of good faith; when you are careless with it, people will feel snubbed. And this doesn't just apply to formal things like invitations to weddings—the size of the event is irrelevant! If you are genuinely unsure if you can attend, don't make the host wait—communicate this to them so they can adjust their expectations and don't feel strung along or dropped at the last minute.

Another unspoken rule is a little like the rule for gifts—you **always say thank you**. Yes, always! You are not thanking the person for the enjoyment you may or may not get out of the occasion. You are thanking them for the courteousness they have shown inviting you. Today, it is a popular hobby to complain loudly and often about how much of an introvert you are and how you cannot bear to go out and socialize. Life is hard; schedules are busy; and people don't always have the energy to get dressed up, leave their homes, and be cheerful and chatty. But then think about it another way: Your host has overcome this understandable inertia and hosted an event anyway. And they were kind enough to consider including you. This is what you thank them for.

If you are attending, great. Say so, ask for any details if you're unsure, and be on time. If you can be there, then there are a few things to bear in mind if you want to say no but with courtesy and consideration. Keep your communications simple, clear, and honest. This means that it is actually quite rude to go on and on at length about all the reasons you can't attend. You might feel nervous or guilty and like you need to explain—but if you overexplain, it comes across as making excuses, and you may cause offense if you continue to labor the point.

Don't make up some colorful lie about why you cannot come—people are very, very good at spotting it. Don't go into detail. It is actually enough to say, "I'm really sorry, but I actually have other commitments that day, so I won't be able to come." If you "protest too much," it starts to look like you consider your attendance some sort of favor to the host. Finally, depending on your relationship to the host, the event, and the context, it may be acceptable to be honest and say that you are simply not up to it. This will work for more casual invites to be with close friends, but will obviously not work when turning down an invitation to a baby christening or a wedding, for example!

Though it might be true, a little white lie about how you're already busy may be the kinder, more polite thing to do. With friends, however, a white lie may seem transparent and unnecessary. You may actually create more trust and rapport by simply saying, "Sorry, guys, I'm feeling a bit exhausted tonight, so I'll give this one a miss. But I'll be along for the next karaoke night!" How do you know which approach to take? Again, consider things from the host's point of view and what will make them feel most respected and considered, then go from there.

Declining a Job Offer

The rule is that the more professional the context, the more important the etiquette rules, and the more of a chance of causing

offense if you ignore them. This is probably most true in the case of dealing with a potential employer or possible client/customer. Don't make the mistake of thinking that it doesn't matter how you treat them since you won't see them again. The truth is, business karma is real and you never know when or how you might encounter that person again! Even if you don't, though, it is a matter of self-respect to treat everyone with consideration no matter if you are directly rewarded for it or not.

If you've been invited to do an interview or you've been offered a job, your first duty is to **be prompt in your response**. Show respect for their time and free them up to look for someone else as soon as possible. Sitting on an offer you know you won't accept is about as rude as "playing the field" when dating!

Secondly, be professional in how you decline. It's almost always best to do so over the phone. As with other invitations, start by thanking the person, and then clearly convey that you cannot accept. Clearness is important—if you're saying no but you're willing to negotiate, this needs to be communicated. If it's a hard no, you need to be clear as well so they don't waste any more time trying to accommodate you. Again, as with other invitations, give a brief explanation but don't overdo it and don't be overly honest. "It's not quite the right role for me at this point" is professional and polite. "To be honest, you're not paying enough and I got bad vibes from the interviewer" is obviously not.

Follow up the conversation with a properly written email, again thanking the hiring manager and interview panel. Express a wish to keep in touch and then wish them luck in their ongoing hiring process. If timing was genuinely an issue, ask to be kept in mind for future openings, if that feels appropriate. Once you've done all this, sit back and relax. There is absolutely no need to ever feel guilty for turning down a job—it happens every day and you are within your rights to do so. Being as polite and conscientious as possible will make the whole thing much easier.

The process is similar for turning down a prospective client or new customer. **Again, the rule is to be prompt, clear, concise, and polite. Explain yourself, but not too much.** If you're turning down business, it's a nice touch to see if you can provide value to the client some other way—refer them to another professional, provide useful information, or point them in the right direction. Never act as though their request is an imposition or that you are above working with them. This way, you turn down that specific request while still maintaining your professional network and keeping the door open so people still feel they can come to you in the future.

Declining Requests

We've already spoken a little about asserting and defending boundaries. Let's take a closer look now at exactly how to say no . . . nicely!

Being both polite and assertive requires a certain mindset shift. Too many of us have been socialized to think of asserting boundaries as a mean, rigid, or cold thing to do. We might think that we have to be doormats to be kind, or that saying no is somehow a risky, awkward, or unlikeable thing to do. Nothing could be further from the truth! Saying no is about respect—for yourself *and* for the other person.

When you say no, you are communicating a clear message to others: You are telling them you know yourself (i.e., your preferences, desires, and limits) and that you have enough self-respect to manage and protect your own resources (such as time, energy, and money). You are also telling them that you respect *them* enough to be clear and honest in what they can expect from you. People tend to appreciate and trust those who honestly assert themselves more than those who are willing to undermine themselves just to avoid awkwardness. Here are a few tips for maintaining assertiveness *and* politeness.

You don't have to respond immediately.

Often, we end up saying yes to things we want to say no to because we feel rushed. But you can always ask for a little time to think about it. It's perfectly okay to say "can I check my calendar first and get back to you?" If you like, you can frame this as for their benefit: "I just want to confirm that I have enough time to give this the attention it deserves."

Stay positive.

It's not the end of the world that you're saying no. Someone else can do it, or the person making the request can think of another way to get their needs met. Beyond that, saying no to their request doesn't mean you can't say yes to something else that suits you better, or agree but on a different timescale. "I can't help you there, I'm afraid, as I'm fully booked all week. But if it helps, I am around the following week?"

This way, you are saying no to that specific request but not no to the general idea of being helpful. Staying positive also means emphasizing that you do in fact value the relationship even if you are saying no in this instance. "I've really had a nice time with you this evening, and I'd love to keep in touch and hang out in class whenever we see each other. But for now, I'd prefer to stay friends."

That said, don't let guilt or awkwardness push you into making promises you don't have any intention of keeping. It's up to you how much you want to keep the door open for future requests.

Give reasons, not excuses.

Be honest and let the other person know a little bit about why you're saying no. But this is just to provide context and a little bit of a buffer—it's not because you need a complicated excuse to justify yourself, and you don't need to ask their permission or launch into a big defense to prove how much you're entitled to say no. You *could* say no and leave it at that, and you'd still be well within your rights. But the extra explanation is a nice courtesy.

Gracefully accept their response.

Bear in mind that they could have a negative response. The hardest part about saying no is realizing that you might inconvenience people or behave in ways they don't want you to.

Nevertheless, their feelings about your reasonable behavior are not your problem to fix. If they're unhappy with a clear boundary of yours, that does not mean it suddenly becomes your job to make them feel better. The most you can do is acknowledge their feelings and stand your ground. "I appreciate that you can't find a babysitter this weekend and that puts you in a tight spot. I have other plans, though, so I'm sorry but I can't help you out."

Many times we fail to say no properly, or we set weak boundaries because we communicate, consciously or unconsciously, that we don't really mean it. We say no, but others know that if they pout and fuss, we will eventually give in. People may push on our guilty feelings or imply that we are obliged or continue asking. It is crucial that we stand our ground no matter what. Whether you are dealing with someone who likes to continually press on boundaries a little or is an outright bully, they cannot get a reaction if you keep presenting your polite refusal like a wall they cannot get past.

The broken record technique helps here: Simply repeat your boundary again and again without changing anything or reacting to any new objections, begging, or pleading. If your boundary is delivered politely and warmly, the other person has no choice but to eventually stop.

"I'm looking after my mother at the moment and I have a lot on my plate, so I'm just not able to give you a lift home each day. I'm sorry!"

"But it won't take much time, don't worry. I only finish a half hour after you, so you won't have to wait long for me."

"Oh, I get that and I understand. But I have to get home and look after my mother."

"Okay, it's just that . . . you were so kind last month and I was kind of counting on you . . ."

"I see that. I'm sorry, but like I said, I can't because I have to take care of my mother."

"Really? I have to say, I'm kind of disappointed. But fine. At least give me a lift today, then, I guess."

"Sorry, but no. I'll need to get home to be there for her."

And so on. Flattery, guilt-tripping, and repeated requests are designed to wear down a boundary. If you continually show that your boundaries are as firm as ever, the person will eventually stop. It's not the most pleasant situation, but the broken record technique is a gentle but effective way to firmly keep out anyone who does not respect your reasonable limits.

Chapter 15: Apology Etiquette

You didn't mean to, but you're only human, and you've done something that's upset someone else. Uh oh—what now? Well, there's good news and bad news. Having to say sorry puts you in a difficult position, but the good news is that if you handle it correctly, your relationship with that person could actually be *stronger* afterward. **That's because a good apology shows maturity, respect, remorse, and a genuine understanding—and that can open doors to a deeper connection with someone.**

The way in which you deliver your apology and the subtle nuances in the language you use play an important part in how it is received. There is no magic in the words "I'm sorry" or "please forgive me." Rather, we convey our sense of regret and true desire to fix things up with everything else that surrounds those words!

The big unspoken rule here, of course, is that you *should* in fact apologize. Never assume that one is not needed. Never assume that you don't have to apologize if you feel bad enough yourself or if it was an accident or if the other person has also hurt you in some way. If you're in the wrong and you've caused harm, then an apology is necessary.

That said, a badly formulated apology can be worse than none at all. We've all experienced that sorry-not-sorry kind of apology that actually inflames hurt feelings. If you've ever started an apology with "I'm sorry, but..." then you already know how utterly useless it is at making other people feel better!

Let's say you asked a friend to stay at their family summer house and they agreed, but asked you to not invite too many others since the place is filled with delicate antiques. You secretly held a party there anyway, and as a result, a drunken guest tripped over a side table and smashed a priceless porcelain vase that belonged to your friend's great-grandmother. There's no two ways around it: You messed up and owe your friend an apology.

Here's how *not* to apologize: You text your friend and tell her the bad news, emphasizing how you never meant it to happen and how awful you feel now, but that it's the other friend's fault and you really hope she can forgive you. Then when she is icy with you, you get irritated and keep asking, "Why are you still upset? What do you want me to do? I can't go back in time, you know!"

Let's look at a better way to do it.

The Six-Step Apology

As it happens, there is a handy formula to make sure that your apology is the best it possibly can be. Roy Lewicki is a professor emeritus of management and human resources at the Fisher College of Business at The Ohio State University, and he claims that there is a narrative framework that every excellent apology ought to follow (Lewicki et al., 2016). Lewicki is a renowned authority on the art of negotiating and spent years studying what constitutes an apology. He came to the realization that it, like any other tale, needed to adhere to a specific structure. When it does, it lands well and smooths over conflict, allowing people to move on. Take a look at the six components he recommends including:

Expression of Regret

First, you need to apologize for your actions. Literally say the words "apologize" or "sorry" so that it's crystal clear what you're doing. Here, tone is important. Whatever you say will seem empty if you're unsympathetic, snarky, or irritated. If you rush, it seems like you don't take the whole thing seriously, so slow down and be polite and sincere.

"Friend, I want to apologize for what I did and let you know how sorry I am."

Explanation of What Went Wrong

It's important not to start with this; otherwise, it may seem like you're making excuses. You're explaining, but you're not excusing, justifying, or defending. This step is not for your benefit but theirs: You want them to know what your intentions were—which were not to hurt them! Try to communicate that things went wrong not because you didn't care or you deliberately intended them harm. This may seem obvious to you, but it's a courteous thing to spell it out deliberately to them.

"I never planned for any of it to happen. I invited Jane over but did not anticipate her getting drunk that evening and never guessed she'd damage something so valuable."

Take Responsibility

If there's one thing that can completely invalidate an apology, it's the feeling that the person doesn't actually believe they are to blame for what's happened. When you are not accountable for the results of your own actions or try to blame others, people will seldom let you off the hook but will rather get annoyed that you are not maturely owning your part in the situation. They may in fact respond with more blame to force you to accept your responsibility.

Instead, be brave, drop your ego and defensiveness, and come clean. Show them that you are genuinely aware of your conduct and how it has affected them. For this step to be achieved, you need to accept *total* responsibility. Even if it is a freak accident out of your control or you didn't mean it, you are still accepting the fact that your actions caused certain consequences.

"Nevertheless, I accept full responsibility for going against your wishes and inviting her. It was my carelessness to blame for the vase being broken."

Declare Your Repentance

People who are wronged feel a sense of injustice. They really want to know that the bad thing is not going to happen again. But of course, it's not satisfying to simply have an empty promise—you have to mean it. "That was the most important factor in our second study," says Lewicki. You need to communicate that you regret what happened and have learned your lesson. If you promise to do something, do it. If you don't, that apology and all others instantly lose their value.

"It's too late to change anything now, but I feel so desperately regretful that I allowed that to happen. I wish now that I had behaved better, but I can only say I have learned my lesson and will never do something so disrespectful to a valued friend ever again. I know that it will take time to trust me again, but I want to give you my word that I will never be so inconsiderate with your kindness again."

Make an Offer for Reparations

Because of the sense of injustice, you can go some way to fixing things by offering to balance the scales again. Show them that you are aware they've been wronged and that you are willing to take steps to compensate them somehow. Granted, this won't always be possible, but to the extent you can, offer to make things right in concrete, valuable ways. You need them to feel that you're not just sorry in the moment but have a real plan to repair things. If people feel like the incident has at least led to improved outcomes in the future, your apology will feel like it's worth a lot more. You could offer to pay for damages, or consider a gift, kind gesture, or token/symbol of your remorse. Importantly, it has to be something *they* value, not you.

"I understand that the vase was not only incredibly expensive, but that it also had sentimental value. Though I realize it doesn't begin to make up for the loss, I have sought a specialist who is able to treat porcelain damage of this kind, and will pay for a full assessment and repair, should you give your permission."

Ask for Forgiveness

Interestingly, this was, according to Lewicki, the least important part of an effective apology. He recommends you lead up to this part and only ask for forgiveness once you've covered all the other steps. Starting with a request for forgiveness is actually asking the other person to do something for you—and to do it without any effort on your behalf.

Instead, ask for forgiveness as a cherry on top. Remember that you are only asking, not demanding. They are not obliged to forgive you, and you'd be unwise to push for it. If they are still angry or upset, then respect that and give them their space. Do not make them feel bad, guilty, or wrong for still being unhappy—that is their prerogative. Even if you give the perfect apology, you cannot predict or control other people's emotions or how they will respond to your remorse. However, the gracious thing to do is always to apologize fully, but only once. Continuing to apologize sets up strained dynamics. Be as sincere as you can, then back off and let time do its work.

"Again, I feel awful about all of this, and I can't imagine how you must feel, but I hope in time you can forgive me."

You might be wondering what form an apology should take. Ideally, you should apologize as soon as possible, but if it's appropriate, it might be worth waiting a little while if it means you can issue a more formal and prepared apology in writing. Waiting a little while also gives you time to gather your thoughts and think about what you can do to make reparations.

Texts or messages relayed through others are a bad idea unless the offense was very, very minor. As far as possible, try to meet in person, or if you're conveying apologies in writing, do some with the proper formality, i.e., send a handwritten note or a properly constructed, grammatically correct email. Depending on the size of the transgression, you might like to send a card plus a small gift, like flowers, chocolates, wine, or something that connects to the issue at hand.

A few things to avoid:

- Passive voice, i.e., talking as though a problem just happened, rather than you were the active agent causing it to happen. For example, say "I'm sorry I hurt you" instead of "I'm sorry you were hurt."
- Expressing how bad *you* feel. You might be feeling completely rotten and eaten up with guilt, but to be honest, this is not really relevant for the other person. The last thing you want to do is make it all about you or even make the other person feel like your response is somehow theirs to deal with on top of the original issue.
- Expecting that you are owed anything just because you apologized. Say sorry

because it's the right thing to do. Then, it's out of your hands. That means that it's not up to you to decide what happens next. Sometimes, the Bad Thing is bad enough to permanently end a relationship or change it in ways you don't like. It's sad, but we cannot get upset with others because of their responses to our actions.
- That said, there's no need to beg and plead and keep on apologizing forever. Say your piece, be better, then move on as much as you can.

One last thing to consider: what's the best way to accept an apology?

Well, if it's offered sincerely and with a genuine intent to make things right, to show remorse, and to repair the relationship, then say thank you and take a moment to decide what you want to do. You can be polite and courteous and still not accept an apology, if that's how you feel. Still, there's a lot to be said for acknowledging anyone's sincere effort to take responsibility for themselves and say sorry. Kindly acknowledge this effort, but it's okay to ask for time to think things over, process your feelings, or get a little space. Making it known that you are unhappy is not rude or inconsiderate—as with all etiquette rules, it's about *how* you do it.

"Hi, friend. I really appreciate that you had the decency to write me an apology for what happened at the summer house, and I'm sure that took courage. Thank you for making inquiries about getting the vase repaired. I value our friendship and I am thankful that you are taking steps to make things right between us. For the next little while, though, I think I would most appreciate some space between us just to let things cool off."

Summary:

- Occasionally "social misfires" do happen but can be managed and mitigated. First, try to avoid giving unsolicited advice—even if suggestions, interpretations, and "lessons" are subtle and well-meaning. Instead of telling people what to do, show non-judgment, compassion, and empathy and just listen.
- Not all social interactions are successful, and not everyone will want to talk/be friends. That's okay. Watch a person's body language and behavior and notice patterns of withdrawal. Gracefully accept rejection without taking it personally.
- You are always entitled to turn down an invitation or request as long as you do so in a way that is sincere, follows proper

protocol, and shows respect for the person asking you. Consider their situation and be respectful.
- When saying no, respond quickly, say thank you, be concise and polite, and give a clear but not overly long explanation. Don't feel guilty or try to compensate. Stay positive, ask for some time to help you decide, and don't allow yourself to be bullied—use the broken record technique if necessary.
- An effective apology contains six components: expressing regret, explaining what went wrong, taking responsibility, declaring repentance, offering reparations, and requesting forgiveness. Likewise, whether you are accepting or rejecting an apology yourself, always be polite and civil.

Summary Guide

Part 1: Making Contact

- Good etiquette, manners, and social skills will make you more likeable, a better conversationalist, and more skilled at diffusing conflict. Social skills are natural, but they're not always easy or automatic!
- Prioritize establishing a shared space of mutual respect, understanding, and good intent. Greetings and introductions matter since they speak to people's needs to belong and be included. Never forget to properly greet people. Formally or informally, greet with **authenticity, presence, and intention**.
- Always introduce strangers from the "bottom up" in formal/professional situations.
- Etiquette rules in public are there to minimize friction. Pay attention, minimize device use, and keep out of people's way. Have situational empathy: Be aware of yourself and of others. When in doubt, behave in a way that puts everyone else most at ease.

- Eye contact equals intimacy. Hold contact for four seconds and try the triangle technique to show interest when listening to others speak. Be aware of the power of eye contact to show sexual interest, as well as cultural contexts. If you're ever unsure, match and mirror other people's eye contact.
- Small talk is an essential part of *gradually* building intimacy. Avoid conversational danger zones: appearances, money, sex, politics, and religion—at least until you know the person better! Gracefully change the topic and keep things moving.
- Finally, don't be the person who is proud to be "blunt"—this is just laziness.

Part 2: The Golden Rule is Respect

- When we are punctual, we are showing respect for people's time. Be prepared by planning your schedule in advance, and proactive in making adjustments as soon as possible to avoid awkwardness. Create a reputation for trustworthiness by keeping your word and doing as you say you will.
- Respect other people's right to be different from you and have their own perceptions,

interpretations, and opinions. Conflict is optional; rise above it. Disagree gracefully, try to hear and reflect the emotional core of what you're told, and listen for universal truths.
- Respect personal space by understanding and respecting the different proximal zones: intimate, personal, social, and public. Be aware of gender and culture differences.
- Generally, the closer the relationship, the smaller the distance, so adjust accordingly. There are strong connections between psychological space and physical proximity. Proximity equals intimacy, so if you change the proxemic zone, you are communicating a change in degree of intimacy.
- Always, always respect a person's boundaries no matter whether or not you agree with, understand, or share their limits. Accept what you're told, don't punish or guilt people, and pay attention to nonverbal communication too.
- Communicate your own boundaries early, clearly, and assertively; don't overexplain or feel guilty; and be willing to follow through.

Part 3: Unspoken Rules of Engagement

- Conversational flow is that state of enjoyment and ease that requires your focus on the other person rather than your own ego.
- Use the principle of inspiration as an invitation to jump start conversational flow. An invitation is saying something that explicitly lets your partner know it is their turn to speak. An inspiration is saying something that makes your partner want to speak without you prompting them.
- The secret to good conversation is to genuinely care and to listen to what you're told. Be receptive and non-judgmental, ask questions, and show interest.
- The rule of reciprocity is the idea that when someone gives you a gift, whether it's an object, a kind deed, or an act of generosity, you automatically repay it or do something nice in return. Generosity is about fortifying the webs of social connection. Always return a favor; family or personal relationships often have more relaxed expectations on that return, but it is still required.
- Gratitude, manners, and kindness all have significant overlap. The more gratitude we show, the better we feel and the less likely we are to take things for granted or complain, and the more likely we are to be grateful. We also increase feelings of

generosity since we are not coming from a place of fear or insecurity. Instead, try random acts of kindness and be aware of and responsive to people's needs.
- Humor is a powerful way to deflect tension. But never use humor to harm others; steer clear of sarcasm, mockery, and contentious topics when making jokes.

Part 4: When Things Don't Go to Plan

- Occasionally "social misfires" do happen but can be managed and mitigated. First, try to avoid giving unsolicited advice—even if suggestions, interpretations, and "lessons" are subtle and well-meaning. Instead of telling people what to do, show non-judgment, compassion, and empathy and just listen.
- Not all social interactions are successful, and not everyone will want to talk/be friends. That's okay. Watch a person's body language and behavior and notice patterns of withdrawal. Gracefully accept rejection without taking it personally.
- You are always entitled to turn down an invitation or request as long as you do so in a way that is sincere, follows proper protocol, and shows respect for the person

asking you. Consider their situation and be respectful.
- When saying no, respond quickly, say thank you, be concise and polite, and give a clear but not overly long explanation. Don't feel guilty or try to compensate. Stay positive, ask for some time to help you decide, and don't allow yourself to be bullied—use the broken record technique if necessary.
- An effective apology contains six components: expressing regret, explaining what went wrong, taking responsibility, declaring repentance, offering reparations, and requesting forgiveness. Likewise, whether you are accepting or rejecting an apology yourself, always be polite and civil.

www.ingramcontent.com/pod-product-compliance
Lightning Source LLC
Chambersburg PA
CBHW020531080526
44583CB00013B/823